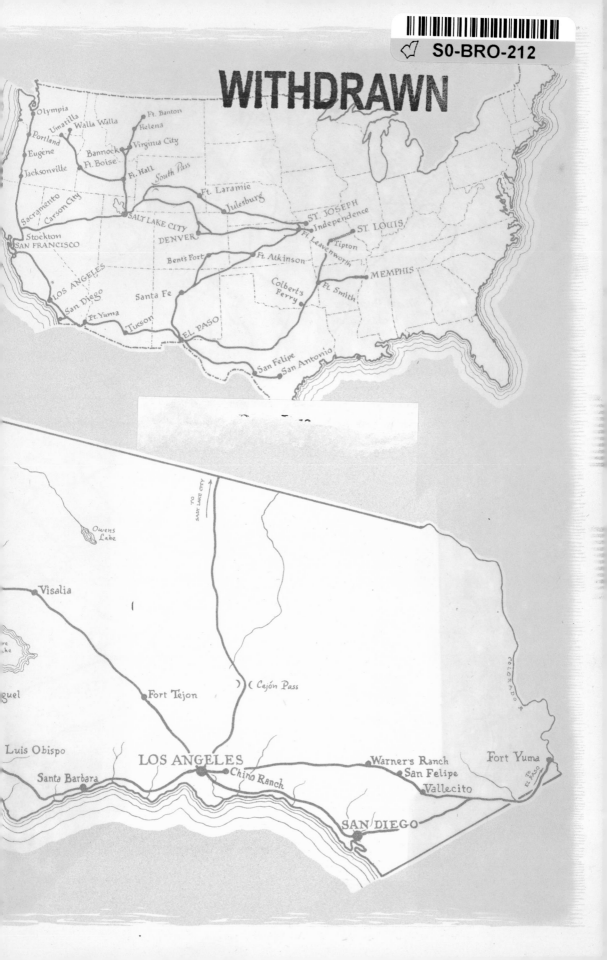

VIA WESTERN EXPRESS
AND STAGECOACH

By OSCAR OSBURN WINTHER

STANFORD UNIVERSITY

VIA
WESTERN
EXPRESS &
STAGECOACH

PRESS *Stanford University, California*

STANFORD UNIVERSITY PRESS, STANFORD UNIVERSITY, CALIFORNIA

THE BAKER AND TAYLOR COMPANY, 55 FIFTH AVENUE, NEW YORK 3, N.Y.
HENRY M. SNYDER & CO., 440 FOURTH AVENUE, NEW YORK 16, N.Y.

First printing, November 1945
Second printing, December 1945

To Mary
who insisted this book
should be entitled
Expressly Yours

". . . . and the driving is like the driving
of Jehu the son of Nimshi; for he driveth
furiously."

2 Kings 9 : 20

PREFACE

THIS IS THE STORY OF STAGECOACH AND express transportation in California before the "Iron Horse" came puffing across the Sierra Nevada.. Also, it is the history of travel during a time when hordes of people from all parts of the globe rushed to California in search of fortune and fame, a time when the West was bumptious, raucous, and wild.

Gold was the magnet that drew thousands upon thousands to the Mother Lode country, far from the established coastal towns and from navigable waters. Providing means of going to and from the diggings, of getting the precious yellow dust to places of safekeeping, of getting letters to homesick miners taxed the ingenuity of the frontier society which mushroomed into being during the quarter-century that followed the discovery of gold by James W. Marshall in 1848.

The subject of this book has many ramifications. The cold, sober statistics, the involved facts and the long list of names and dates, and the analysis of economic trends connected with the transportation business—subjects stressed in my *Express and Stagecoach Days in California* (Stanford University Press, 1936, 1938)—have been reduced here to a minimum. Instead, the emphasis has been placed upon the more human, the more picturesque and exciting aspects of overland transportation. The modes, dangers, hardships, and delights of cross-country travel, wayside taverns and their bills-of-fare, pioneer stage and express men, famous drivers, and notorious highwaymen have received the main emphasis.

And, lastly, I have sought to show the extent to which California was isolated from the rest of the nation and what was done in the pre-railroad age to improve communication and the handling of the mails between the Golden State and her sister commonwealths in the East. The stories of the Butterfield Overland Mail, the Pony Express, Russell, Majors and Waddell, Ben Holladay, and Wells, Fargo and Company bring the book to its conclusion.

I have been greatly assisted in this work by Frances Hathaway Hyde, research assistant, and by Mary Winther, and am deeply grateful to them. I am also indebted to Catherine Harroun, historian of the Wells Fargo Bank and Union Trust Company Historical Museum, for the many illustrations which she has kindly placed at my disposal. Moreover, I owe a debt of gratitude to Indiana University for making time, funds, and facilities available to me while doing the writing. And, of course, this book would not have been possible without the historical records provided in many libraries, which institutions I acknowledge individually in my Bibliographical Note.

O. O. W.

Henry E. Huntington Library
San Marino, California
November 1, 1945

CONTENTS

ILLUSTRATIONS

Decorative illustrations by
ARTHUR LITES

Chapter I

GOLD! GOLD! GOLD!

IT WAS A RAINY JANUARY EVENING IN 1848, when the gaunt and wild-eyed James Wilson Marshall arrived at Sutter's Fort at New Helvetia, California. Marshall was "dripping with water," and was very much excited. He asked to see his employer, the baronial John Sutter, "alone." Sutter appeared and invited Marshall into a private room.

"Are you alone?" asked Marshall. "Did you lock the door?"

Upon being assured of privacy, the nervous visitor drew a dripping rag from his pocket and held it before Sutter. It contained, wrote Sutter, "what might have been an ounce and a half of gold dust—dust, flakes and grains."

"I believe this is gold; but the people at the mill laughed at me and called me crazy."

"Yes," admitted Sutter, "it certainly looks like it; we will try it."

It was gold; no doubt about it.

On January 24, just four days previously, Marshall had been at work constructing a sawmill for Sutter on the south fork of the American River. He had glanced into the tailrace of the mill and, observing the particles, had collected them and brought them to Sutter.

Sutter was not anxious to have the news of this discovery spread, and for various reasons it was early May before the great excitement began. Then it was that tiny and sleepy San Francisco was suddenly stirred by Sam Brannan, a shrewd Mormon merchant from Sacramento. In the pueblo market-place and before a curious group of listeners, Brannan flashed a small bottle of

1

"dust" in one hand and waved his hat with the other. What he said is not known, but the effect of Brannan's demonstration was electrifying. With this cry the great California Gold Rush really got under way. The news spread like wildfire among California's 20,000 inhabitants, who only a week after Marshall's discovery had changed allegiance from Mexico to the United States. San Francisco, then a town of about 1,000, literally closed shop as all its able-bodied males hustled off toward Coloma, the scene of the discovery, in search of gold. So many left the Santa Clara Valley for the diggings during the summer of 1848 that the region was not sufficiently protected from the depredations of Indians and outlaws. Even the crops sown during the preceding winter were left unharvested, while cattle, horses, and hogs were turned loose to graze at will upon the fields of grain. "I can get no hands on acc't of the Gold fever, which increases daily," wrote a native of San Jose in June. "Wagons & pack animals are constantly passing thitherward."

Within a one-week period in June over 1,000 men left Monterey for the mines. Only an occasional loyal soldier and a gang of prisoners remained to comprise the male population of the once-active Spanish capital. It had become, wrote one, "a community of women."

As the fever spread southward, the effect was the same; the coastal towns of Santa Barbara, Los Angeles, and San Diego became all but depopulated.

There were no roads to speak of—merely trails connecting one settlement or rancho with another. But that did not deter the gold-fevered Californians, who proceeded hastily to blaze new routes wherever they were needed. Most of the local men preferred traveling to the new mines on horseback; but there were some who went with wagons, on foot, or by whatever means seemed most expedient at the time.

Meanwhile the news spread to Hawaii, to Oregon, to Mexico; by September it reached the eastern states; and soon it was loudly heralded throughout the entire world. Story followed story about fantastic discoveries.

"We have accounts of the discovery of the most wonderful gold mine on record," wrote the *Indiana State Sentinel*, September 27, 1848.

"As regards the richness of these Mines, I can only say that the most exaggerated accounts may be believed," added a correspondent for the *New York Tribune*.

And the *Cincinnati Gazette* chimed in: "Indeed, if all reports be true, the whole earth is mixed with it for hundreds of miles, the extent of which has not yet been ascertained, and there cannot be a scarcity of the article for a thousand years to come."

The climax came on December 5, 1848, when President James K. Polk announced to Congress that "the accounts of the abundance of gold" in California were "corroborated by the authentic reports." Then it was that the gold fever reached a high pitch throughout the nation.

People everywhere prepared to leave for California—by way of Cape Horn, by one of the land routes over Mexico or the Isthmus, or overland across the "Great American Desert." Those who decided to go by either of the first two routes could leave as soon as ships were available; but those wishing to go overland were obliged to wait for the favorable weather of the spring of 1849.

The first immigrants to reach California after the discovery of gold came over the land-water route. They had found passage to Chagres and had crossed the Isthmus to Panama, where they boarded the Pacific Mail Steamship Company steamer, *California,* then making its maiden voyage to the West Coast. The vessel left New York before the excitement struck, and when it steamed into Panama, over 1,500 frantic people were awaiting passage to San Francisco. Only about 400 of these could be taken aboard, the fare being $1,000 for each person. The *California* docked at the Golden Gate port on February 28, 1849, and this day marks the coming of the first 'Forty-niners. From then on California was to experience a phenomenal growth in population.

By late summer long caravans from across the parched plains and the Sierra Nevada began arriving, and the population swelled by leaps and bounds. By the end of the year the population exceeded the 100,000 mark.

The greatest mushroom town of all was San Francisco, formerly the tiny, somnolent pueblo Yerba Buena. After sustaining its mass exodus to the mines it began growing in what might well be termed wildest disorder.

In the wake of the *California* scores of other vessels began pouring into San Francisco Bay to disgorge their thousands of passengers and their freight. By November 1849 over 500 vessels at anchor in the Bay could be counted. While most ships' passengers hurried off immediately to the mines, many wise men remained in this port town to establish themselves in business. Miners needed supplies. Would-be San Francisco merchants knew this and realized that the surest way to get rich was to remain in San Francisco and let others dig the gold. By August the city's population had bounced to 20,000.

Not only did San Francisco become a great boom city; it became a city of shanties. Its hastily-erected homes and stores rested precariously, it seemed, upon the sand hills off the bay. Fires were frequent and devastating; but again and again the city bounded back—bigger, busier, livelier than before. "Stretching its youthful limbs in the gusty air," says the historian, H. H. Bancroft, "San Francisco grew apace . . . . carving the slopes into home sites for climbing habitations till they reached the crests, leveling the hills by blasting out ballast for returning vessels, or material for filling in behind the rapidly advancing piling in the cove." San Francisco became a city of bad planning but one with a soul and a cosmopolitan spirit that epitomized the great Gold Rush excitement.

As a matter of fact, more than one-half of the immigrants chose to remain in the cities, particularly San Francisco, Sacramento, San Jose, and Stockton. All these towns became important base-cities, and as such their chief function was supplying far-off mining camps with food and equipment. It was in the conduct of these operations that critical problems of transportation soon arose.

When the Gold Rush began, a stagecoach, let alone a railroad, was a luxury unknown among Mexicans, and to the American gold seekers these were but a romantic memory of the comfortable life back home. Instead, the first arrivals in California found the Mexican *carreta* still in use. They saw with impatience its two clumsy wheels being slowly inched forward, either by a stodgy ox or by a balky, lazy mule. If their own backs were to be spared, the Argonauts soon discovered that, for the long hauls from entrepôts to diggings, sole dependence had to be placed upon long strings of

Mexican mules. These were, as one wrote, "a kind of connecting link between the vallies and the mountains." Men soon came to welcome the muleteers' echoing cries of "Hippah, mulah," as a pack train approached a camp or bar. Not until months had elapsed did wagon freighting and stagecoaching begin.

Beautiful San Francisco peninsula provided the first testing ground for stagecoach transportation. Along the bay shore the land was flat. Aged, gnarled oaks on mountains near by added a magnificent grandeur to what in dry weather was a natural roadway that stretched from the Golden Gate to San Jose—California's oldest pueblo.

It was over this fifty-mile stretch that "get-aheadative" John Whistman offered to the public regular nine-hour stagecoach service in the early autumn of 1849. But, in the opinion of at least one contemporary, this service was not first class. Such an opinion was probably justified, since Whistman's equipment consisted of an old French omnibus driven by poorly groomed mustangs and mules. At the end of his run, Whistman simply turned his animals loose to graze; and an eyewitness reports that a mere corral served as a stable. Since this pioneer entrepreneur made no promises as to how often he would make the nine-hour trek, it is believed that he held to it only when the weather remained fair.

Even in California it rains. And when the wet season of the year came, the ground became "so soft that wheels soon sank to the hubs." Whistman, compelled to change his route, made Alviso, situated on the southern tip of San Francisco Bay, his northern terminus for the rainy season. At Alviso, San Jose passengers made connections with steamboats for San Francisco and other places in the Bay.

Whistman re-established his original route in the spring of 1850. The fare of thirty-two dollars or "two ounces," which he charged, soon interested others in what seemed to be a very remunerative enterprise. And so it happened that, in April, Whistman faced his first competition. A new concern, known as Ackley and Maurison, had established a triweekly service over the same route. Certainly this was a situation Whistman could scarcely ignore. No more old nags and makeshift wagons for the peninsula. Ackley and Maurison's line was "furnished with the best stages and horses the country can produce." This proved too much for Whistman, who sold his business to Warren F. Hall and Jared B. Crandall in the summer of 1850. These two men, previously engaged in staging in Mexico, had sufficient means and experience to equip and operate a stagecoach line. Like their competitors, Ackley and Maurison, they at once offered regular service; and it was not long before they became popular and influential figures in the staging business of northern California.

In May 1851, Hall and Crandall, competing with several bidders, were awarded a four-year contract to carry the mails of the United States between San Francisco and San Jose three times a week. The terms of the contract provided for the use of four-horse coaches, for which the government granted a compensation of $6,000 per annum.

On July 2, 1851, Hall and Crandall announced that the fare on their line between San Francisco and San Jose had been reduced from thirty-two to sixteen dollars and that stages would leave each terminal every morning. They also gave notice that their line had been extended to Monterey, with a stage leaving San Jose every Monday and Thursday and arriving there the following evening. Thus did restive San Franciscans witness a rapid improvement in their peninsular transportation.

This schedule established by Hall and Crandall remained in effect for the remainder of 1851 and all through the next year. The partners begged the public to take advantage of their "reduced rate" and "visit the beautiful and healthful valley of Santa Clara," stating that a "more charming drive" was not to be found in California. As one is "whirled rapidly through the oak openings and across the level plains under the skillful driving of Professors Dillon or Crandal [sic], who drive their coaches, he finds that pleasure is united with business, and wonders he has never made the trip before." In April 1853, Hall and Crandall sold their line to Dillon, Hedge and Company and became interested in the development of stagecoach lines in other parts of the state.

San Francisco was by no means the sole center of attention. The city of Sacramento likewise developed and soon spread widely over acres which until 1849 had been tilled leisurely by the Swiss John Sutter.

The history of staging in and around Sacramento is therefore similar to that on the San Francisco peninsula, except that the first lines were established by an entirely different group of men. Into the future capital came two adventurous and enterprising young men—James Birch and Frank Stevens. These two amiable and resourceful persons had arrived in California in 1849 as members of an overland immigrant party. They hailed from New England where both had "driven stage," and it was not long after their arrival at Sacramento that they again turned to a type of work they enjoyed.

Neither of them had much capital. James Birch began operations with no better equipment than John Whistman; but Birch possessed far greater skill and business sense than his San Francisco contemporary. In September 1849, seated upon an old *rancho* wagon drawn by four Mexican broncos, Birch began his California career. He offered to carry passengers from Sacramento to Mormon Island, on the south fork of the American River. The fare thirty-two dollars or, if one did not have the cash, a couple of ounces of dust.

Just what James Birch did to improve and expand his business is not definitely known. A Birch advertisement, dated February 10, 1850, announced "Through by Daylight!" service from Sacramento to Mormon Island and Sutter's Mill at Coloma. The service was daily, including Sundays; and the drivers were to be none other than Birch himself and A. Briggs.

The press kept the public well informed on Birch's enterprise, and on March 9th the Sacramento *Placer Times* made the following revealing comment:

"We made an 'experimental trip' in one of Mr. Birch's stages a few days ago, which proved highly satisfactory. The horses had never been harnessed but once or twice before, yet they dashed through sloughs and gulches in a remarkably knowing style. These California horses seem to know about as much as most folks. The appearance of the country in the vicinity of the Fort is very pleasing: flowers being in bloom and cultivation going forward with a good deal of activity. The party returned highly delighted with the hour's ride, and fully satisfied that Birch's Line was *the* line to get to the Mines in a hurry."

In 1851 Birch's name appears among the bidders for a government contract to carry mails out of Sacramento, and in the same year he organized the Telegraph Line of United States Mail

Stages, which, with headquarters at Sacramento, made daily rounds through such important mining towns as Rough and Ready, Grass Valley, and Nevada City. He also extended his line from Sacramento to Stockton in the same year.

During his first three years in California Stevens confined his efforts largely to the hotel and tavern business, and only incidentally did he go into staging. Later he shifted his emphasis, and in 1851 he founded the Pioneer Line of stages to serve Sacramento and Placerville (Hangtown). Stevens and Birch became closely associated and apparently did not compete with each other. Together the two men soon made staging service of the finest style available to most of the northern mines, going far up the north Yreka River to Foster's Bar, to other camps on the south Yuba, and to places along the important American River.

North of the city of Sacramento the trails and crude roads led toward Shasta City and mining camps on the upper Sacramento River, and Marysville on the Feather River. It was a farmer named John Sharp who first began a crude stage line between Sacramento and Marysville. Then, in 1851, the up and coming Hall and Crandall concern moved into this new province, and their first step was to buy out Sharp.

This modest beginning was only part of a plan calling for service to Shasta City, a distance of 180 miles north of Sacramento. Such a program was very ambitious, for in 1849 the only road between Sacramento and Shasta City was a mule trail used in earlier days by the Hudson's Bay Company. All supplies, express, and mails had been brought into Shasta City during 1849-1850 by pack-mule trains. But by 1851 Hall and Crandall had found a passable road, and with stock taken from their large ranch in Santa Clara County they inaugurated a stagecoach line to this distant northern town on the upper Sacramento River.

Since steamboat service was available on the Sacramento River as far as Colusa, it became customary for passengers from Sacramento to the Siskiyou region to travel by water to Colusa and there take a stage for the rest of the way. In the autumn of 1851 the water level of the rivers was at such a low point that travel by ship north of Sacramento was suspended and, luckily for the stage men, coaches were used exclusively.

Within two years Hall and Crandall operated stages over 300

miles of California's roads, and in the Sacramento advertisements they could boast the daily departure and return of several six-horse teams, "speed and comfort . . . . unsurpassed in the world," and the sparing of no pains to procure the "BEST HORSES, finest CONCORD COACHES, and the most competent and CAREFUL DRIVERS."

It is apparent that by 1851 Sacramento, rather than San Francisco, had become the most important center of stagecoach travel, a supremacy which it was to retain during the 'fifties. According to the *Alta California* of November 12, 1851, several lines were operating out of Sacramento on that date as follows: six daily to Marysville; one to Nevada City; two to Coloma; one to Placerville; one to Auburn; one to Stockton (also one triweekly line); and one to Drytown and Jackson.

The stages were "punctual and regular in the hours of departure and arrival, unless delayed by bad roads," according to the *Alta California's* Sacramento correspondent, and "to look upon their crowded coaches as they roll along . . . . we are fully convinced that our proprietors are well paid for the part they perform." He placed the average number of passengers at seventy daily each way between Sacramento and Marysville; while he states that the Nevada City stage carried "eleven inside," and the Stockton stage usually had its "full complement."

During the years 1852 and 1853 the stagecoach business continued to expand. The old routes were being lengthened and at least one new important road was added to those already established in November 1851. Charles Green opened a stage route between Sacramento and Sonora by way of Ione Valley, Jackson, and Columbia in April 1853; thus for the first time a line of stage travel between the northern and southern mines was established which cut straight across the eastern tributaries of the Sacramento and San Joaquin rivers. "For information," reads Green's ad, "see Agents . . . . who will attend particularly to waking up passengers or otherwise notifying them of the time of departure."

Bancroft estimates that twelve stage lines terminated at Sacramento in March 1853, each using from thirty-five to 150 horses. The total capital of the combined lines he placed at $335,000.

Among the centers of the stagecoach travel in California before 1854 the new and thriving town of Stockton is important. No staging business had been established in 1849 in Stockton because most of those going to the southern mines traveled by water to that city and walked or rode on horseback or muleback to their destination. The first passenger service of any description in or out of Stockton was carried on in 1850 by E. S. Holden in conjunction with a freighting business between there and Sonora. All that is known of this project is that Holden offered to transport passengers to the mines. During the early part of 1851, Kelly, Reynolds and Company was organized and not only acquired the Holden freighting interests but also established the first real daily stage line out of Stockton.

By July 1851, the Telegraph (Stage) Line from Sacramento had reached Stockton, and soon afterward three other concerns, Fisher and Company, Bodge, Ready and Company, and J. Brown and Company, were established with headquarters at this gateway to the southern mines. During 1852 Alonzo McCloud started a line to compete with Kelly, Reynolds and Company, and other staging concerns extended their original routes to include almost all the towns in the region of the southern mines.

The concentration of the mining industry in an area lying east and north of San Francisco prevented San Diego, Los Angeles, Santa Barbara, and other southern communities from enjoying the same increase in population as their neighbors to the North. Both the express and the stage business developed slowly in these old but small mission towns. Not until 1852 was the first stagecoach company organized in this area, when Phinias Banning, later a famous "whip," and D. W. Alexander opened a stage route between Los Angeles and San Diego. Others soon appeared. The next year J. L. Tomlinson established another line to compete with Banning and Alexander, and before the close of 1853 stage connections were made for the first time between the two sections of the state by way of San Luis Obispo, Santa Barbara, and San Buenaventura.

The transportation situation thus far was one in which free enterprise dominated. The number of operators was large, the routes were short (usually less than one hundred miles each), and competition was of the ruinous variety.

Then, late in 1853, there came a change. A number of the most prominent stage-line proprietors, led by Birch, Stevens, Green,

Hall, and Crandall, took steps to effect a consolidation of all major lines in northern California with headquarters at Sacramento.

On January 1, 1854, a merger was announced officially. The name given the new organization was the California Stage Company. This deal was one of the most important business developments in California during the early 'fifties, and can be compared only with its counterpart, the California Steam Navigation Company.

James Birch, who five years earlier had begun from scratch, was now chosen president of the firm, which was capitalized at $1,000,000. His pal, Stevens, was made vice-president. Charles McLaughlin, another up-and-coming stage man, was made general superintendent. Headquarters were established at the Orleans Hotel in Sacramento, and without further ado the new company was open for business.

It has been stated that this important merger absorbed at least five-sixths of all the stage lines in California, which meant a virtual monopoly of the stagecoach business in the northern part of the state. Assets consisted largely of material equipment, including 750 horses, and the coaches, harness, and fixtures necessary to take care of a route at least 450 miles long.

In January 1855, a year after its establishment, the California Stage Company for the first time extended its lines into territory lying south of San Francisco, with the purchase of the interests of two companies. The first was the Dillon, Hedge and Company line (the old Whistman and Hall and Crandall route) running between San Francisco, San Jose, and Monterey; the other was the line of J. A. Talmadge, running between Oakland and San Jose, via Mission San Jose.

Probably in an effort to eliminate all competition, James Birch, president of the company, announced a new schedule of rates, far below any previously advertised, which went into effect on January 11, 1855. The fare, for example, from Sacramento to Mud Springs, Diamond Springs, or Placerville was reduced to three dollars, that to Coloma or Auburn to five dollars, that to Iowa Hill to eight dollars, and that to Yankee Jim's to eleven dollars.

By the time the financial panic hit California in February 1855, the staging business was on a very firm basis. In recognition of the progress which had been made in stagecoach travel Governor

John Bigler addressed the California State Legislature in his annual message, January 5, 1855, as follows: "Inland travel between all the principle parts of the State by means of stages, has .... been rendered expeditious and comfortable. Indeed, California today can boast of stage and coach conveyance equal, if not superior, to any of her sister States."

The transformation of simple, pastoral Spanish California had been amazingly rapid. Within this span of four years, slow, ponderous methods of transportation had given way to stagecoaches drawn by galloping, prancing horses. Roads were not good, but they were well laid out to serve mining camps in remote recesses of the high Sierra Nevada. Cities had sprung up on the Bay and on navigable streams out of which these roads led and from which weekly, thrice weekly, and even daily stagecoach service was offered to a population very much on the move.

Gold! Gold! Gold from the American River! Yes, those were the magic words most responsible for the new day that had dawned in California.

Chapter 2

ALL ABOARD!

HE CALIFORNIA TRAVELER OF 1849 could not be particular. He had to be thankful for anything that moved on wheels. Even John Whistman's rickety old French omnibus was a welcome sight to travelers on the San Francisco peninsula. After all, itchy-footed wayfarers could afford to be just a little patient. Were there not more than enough splendid Concord coaches being made by the Abbott-Downing Company back at Concord, New Hampshire? Would it not be a mere matter of months before latest-model stagecoaches drawn by four- and six-horse teams would be rolling over California's sandy soil?

And what wonderful coaches they were, of most sturdy construction, built to resist the wear, tear, and shock of bumpy frontier roads. Their graceful oval-shaped bodies rested upon two immensely thick thorough-braces, stout leather straps, slung between the front and the rear axles. These made the coaches superior to the common spring wagons, which tended to bounce passengers skywards when a wheel hit a rut—and the ruts were numerous. The Concord coach far surpassed the mud wagon, which had no springs to cushion the bumps. The effect of the thorough-braces was to give a swinging and swaying motion, which Mark Twain aptly characterized as that of a "cradle on wheels."

The body of the Concord—it weighed a ton or more—was so strong that, in addition to accommodating nine passengers inside on three upholstered seats, it provided room for at least a dozen more on the top. Moreover, beside the bumptious driver usually sat either a "shotgun messenger" or some traveling dignitary.

Under the driver's seat there was a place for the treasure box; and extending outward at the rear was a "boot"—a leather-covered rack made to hold mail, express, and baggage. All in all, a Concord coach was a sumptuous yet functional vehicle, and Americans the country over never ceased to admire the beautiful and solid craftsmanship here exhibited by the famous Abbott-Downing firm.

Not all stage operators, especially beginners, could afford Concords, because they cost from $1,200 to $1,500 each, delivered in California. Not all wanted them either, because during the wettest season of the year and over stretches in the high mountains the lighter, low-slung mud wagon was more serviceable. Indeed, sleds were often used for mountain travel during the winter season.

In any event, coaches of one type or another became numerous in California during 1850, and three years later one correspondent counted no less than sixty-seven coaches operating in and out of the busy staging center of Sacramento. Throughout the stagecoach era, the Concord remained the queen of the coaches, and nearly every self-respecting operator in the valley and coastal portion of the state advertised that he owned Concord coaches pulled by either four- or six-horse teams.

Whatever the type of coach used over California's rough roads, traveling could not be done with the optimum of comfort. But even so, it had its charms, its interests, and its excitements. Let us see.

The time is early morning, August 3, 1850, the place San Francisco, the destination San Jose. Out on the Grand Plaza, now known as Portsmouth Square, stands a Berford and Company Waverly omnibus with damask cushions. To it is hitched a fine six-mule team. Twelve passengers have scrambled into the coach, and it's time to go.

"All aboard! All right behind?" asks Dawson, the "whip," as he casts a backward glance at his coach and passengers. "Keep your feet off the seats." Then, "Let her go, Johnny!" And off they trot through the sand hills in a morning "as fine as a cotton hat."

One of our passengers is a correspondent, and while his experiences are fresh in mind, he jots down notes:

"Oh, that sand! Well, we are through it, and there the old Mission breaks upon our view, with its quaint old chapel and the residences of the olden time; its bright, smart, new cottages, rearing their sharp roofs and red chimney tops; the fields, bearing the fresh fruits of the husbandman's toil; the waving hedges, the gentle, trickling streamlets, meandering through the streets and irrigating the 'sarce' gardens; the plain stretching down toward the creek and the bay, relieved by the mountains in the background; and the high road, winding and stretching out until lost in distant hills."

Dawson, "that prince of drivers," has now reached the hard level road heading southward toward San Jose. Soon a little town comes into sight where a change of teams is to be made. The mules know it and without coaxing gallop to the stable and station. But let our correspondent continue in his own words.

"The 'degos' lazily regard the equipage, the Senoritas smile and clap their hands, the little sun-burned, barefooted *niños* shout with their tiny voices; and the doors of the *'Cabeza del Toro'* and the *'Mansion House'* are filled with hombres, who rush out to see the stage come in; the lame hostler hobbles down to his horses, and even the *padre* peeps out to take a look at the new arrival."

A fresh team has been hitched. It is time to leave again. Our correspondent assures us that from now on we shall experience California stage driving at its best.

"Who-a-who-a, there!" shouts Dawson. "Stand by that nigh leader! Now, then, all right! Let 'em go!"

"Whack! Whiz! Whew! we're off to a certainty!" jots down the newsman.

"G-long! crack; h—up, there!" shouts the man on the box.

"A railroad to San Jose! a fiddlestick's end. Not with such a stage as that."

"Look out for that sharp turn there!"

The coach now whirls along over a splendid stretch of road. Soon it reaches the Sanchez ranch, where another change of teams is made. This switch of teams takes only five minutes, and off the coach goes again. During the shift the "Opposition" passed, and Dawson does not like this a bit. A San Francisco-bound coach is met and soon vanishes in the trail of dust. A fourth coach comes up from the rear. What is this anyway? A challenge? You want a race, do you? Dawson has accepted the challenge. He raises his whip.

"Crack, crack, crack! sounds the driver's whip, the wheels hum again—you couldn't want fence posts if they were two rods apart. . . . . The excitement spreads—the most perfect confidence exists in the skill of the driver, who proves himself to be a 'model whip' and as careful as a hen of her chickens. . . . . Every increase of speed is hailed with exclamations of gratification—the spirit of 'fastness' prevails throughout the crowd, ..."

Who won the race, if it really was a race, was not told. We know that Dawson pushed forward at an efficient speed. Every ten or twelve miles a shift of teams was made, but the driver stayed on for the full length of the run. At Captain Wysman's ranch, fourteen miles from San Jose, Dawson stopped to allow his passengers to partake of refreshments—a bowl of rich milk, fresh bread and butter, and California beef and mutton.

Soon Mission Santa Clara comes into view. "All over the Mission lands," writes our correspondent, "persons have reared little tenements with a determination to squat and put in for farms. From the Mission to the outskirts of the Capital, over three miles, is a magnificent *alameda,* composed of a thick grove of luxuriant willows, shading the entire length and breadth of this unsurpassed mall." What he does not seem to know is that these trees had been planted by San Jose's earlier *pobladores* in order to shade them when going to and from Mass at Mission Santa Clara.

Now Dawson's stage rolls into San Jose. He has covered the fifty-mile drive in from five to six hours, including stops. "We have not experienced so much pleasure for some time as we did in our recent fast ride to the Capital of California."

By the autumn of 1850 San Jose had recovered from the mass exodus to the mines the preceding year. Many of its citizenry soon came to realize that the real El Dorado was to be found not at the diggings but in their own back yards. Huge profits could be made selling supplies to those proceeding to the mines from San Francisco by a land route around the shore of the Bay. As inhabitants of the newly created state capital, and in order to meet the requirement of a host, the townspeople were rushing the construction of a two-story adobe State House on the east side of Market Plaza.

California was admitted into the Union on September 9, 1850, and soon the state officials began arriving in San Jose to take office. Competing stage lines vied for the honor of transporting distinguished gentlemen, especially Governor Peter H. Burnett, who traveled there from San Francisco on the morning following Admission Day.

The Governor tells us that he chose a Hall and Crandall stage. On that rare occasion the celebrated "Bob" Crandall did the driving, and the "Gov" occupied the top front seat beside the "Professor." Burnett was proud of Crandall and referred to him as "a most excellent man, and a cool, kind, but determined and skillful driver."

The "Opposition" chose this as a time to really test Crandall's speed. And, according to the Governor, "there was some of the most rapid driving that I ever witnessed. . . . . As we flew past on our rapid course, the people flocked to the road to see what caused our fast driving and loud shouting. . . . . I can never forget Crandall's race. He beat his competitor only a few minutes."

To the Governor and his imbibitory "Legislature of a Thousand Drinks," as well as to the general traveling public, San Jose had little to offer by way of tavern accommodations. There was the City Hotel just opposite Pat Welch's livery stable, but it was terribly overcrowded. Eggs were served at breakfast, at fifty cents apiece. Potatoes were often offered as the main course at dinner, at prices set at two dollars per plate.

Not until the middle 'fifties could the city boast of several hostelries and such exotic attractions as Madam Martin's Hotel de Bordeaux, where good food and the choicest of wines, liquors, cigars, and even a billiard table were made available to guests. And if Madam Martin's hospitality was not desired, then that of Mansion House, the Clinton House, or the Price Hotel might satisfy. The latter served guests, or at least boasted of so doing, "in a style of comfort not to be surpassed by any Hotel in this city. The Table is lavishly supplied with the best viands and all other luxuries the market affords."

The situation was not greatly different near Sutter's Fort, where the new city of Sacramento had sprung into being. Nature favored Sacramento as it did San Francisco. Its prospects for becoming an important inland city were excellent. It was located on the navigable Sacramento River, it lay astride important inland trails, and its proximity to the northern mines promised to make it an important supply center. During January 1849 numerous business houses and dwellings arose in the neighborhood of Sutter's old fort. By June, eleven wholesale houses could be counted along the embarcadero, bearing such names above their doors as Brannan, Whitlock, Gibson, Gillespie, and Taber. Soon the names of Stanford, Hopkins, and Huntington were to appear in the new city's business directory. Real-estate prices began to skyrocket. Lots at first held at $50 to $200 were, by the middle of 1849, offered at $1,000 to $3,000. Meanwhile, sailing vessels and steamers began tying up along its river bank. By June, eighty-five seagoing vessels were anchored there, and from then on Sacramento was an important California port. Soon, too, stagecoaches began rumbling in increasing numbers through the streets of this mushroom city, and by the middle of 1850 her 7,000 inhabitants (many of whom lived in tents) felt they were a part of an emerging metropolitan center. Fires ravaged parts of the city from time to time, and floods came and left their wreckage; but Sacramento rebounded with the speed becoming to a vigorous frontier community.

By far the largest number of California's overland travelers passed in and out of Sacramento. Throughout the gold-rush period it was from Sacramento that the great mass of miners fanned out toward widely scattered diggings and towns of northern California. The distance between San Francisco and this thriving staging center, less than one hundred miles, was nearly always covered by means of Sacramento River steamers. So, too, were points northward that bordered on the upper Sacramento and Feather rivers. With these exceptions, that is, until the coming of railroads, northern California travelers procured their best connections and best services from the staging concerns of Sacramento.

If a traveler of 1851 planned to board a coach from Sacramento for some town in the northern mines, he might have spent the night before his journey in the Crescent Hotel, a hostelry of seventy-five rooms. Long before dawn he would be called to a breakfast by candlelight, a meal which perhaps consisted of beans, venison, and coffee. At break of day he would go to the front of

Old village on the hill near New Almaden
mines about 1862

The New Almaden stage, 1862

San Francisco from the head of Sacramento Street in 1854
(from a lithograph in *Annals of San Francisco*)

the hotel and stage office, where, "fronting one way," a score or more of coaches would be standing, "each behind four restive horses, at whose heads stood grooms holding them in check."

Since the names of the towns to which the stages were going were painted on each vehicle, and the drivers were in the habit of calling out their routes, the traveler would experience little difficulty in locating the right coach. As soon as passengers were seated, the driver would mount his box, cast a "critical glance over the riggings," swear at the horses, make a few adjustments, gather up the "ribbons," utter such a familiar cry as "All aboard for Brighton, Mormon Island, Mud Springs, and Hangtown!" and then off the coach would go "amidst shouts and cracking of whips, and clatter of the horses' feet, and the rattling of stages, through the town, and out into the fresh morning air."

Travelers seemed generally to have enjoyed riding on the stages, although sometimes they did not. Sir Henry Huntley, a British traveler, has left his impressions of a journey from Sacramento to Placerville. Sir Henry complained about the absence of classes, or "divisions," aboard the stages. The passenger, he wrote, "coolly gets into the vehicle and, placing himself between two others, sits down, and relies upon his own weight making the other two sufficiently uncomfortable to aid him in establishing himself between them." Sir Henry was also annoyed, as were so many Britishers, by the unceremonious use of tobacco by "dirty citizens;" and, lastly, he was distracted when one stage met another and greetings were exchanged in "language that places blasphemy . . . . as a light offense, comparatively." The road to Placerville was the best over which Huntley had gone; for about twenty-five miles of it lay across plains and the remainder was a "gradual ascent, each mountain increasing in magnitude, till, through the forest of straggling oaks and pines mingled together, the heights over Placerville" were reached.

A much more inviting account of stage travel out of Sacramento has been left by J. D. Borthwick. "To sit behind four horses tearing along a good road is delightful at any time," states this Britisher, "but the mere fact of such rapid locomotion formed only a small part of the pleasure of our journey. . . . . The atmosphere was so soft and balmy," he continued, "that it was a positive enjoyment to feel it brushing over one's face like the finest floss silk."

With each passing year Sacramento expanded its staging business. In 1853, one newspaperman counted at this city the daily coming and going of about 300 stagecoach passengers. Then, as we have seen, came the formation of the California Stage Company. This brought with it an enlargement of the staging facilities and a still greater increase in patronage. Somehow the formation of the California Stage Company as a monopoly failed to bring the scorn and censure usually accompanying such developments. "This company," wrote the Sacramento *State Journal,* "is the first monopoly that we ever met that succeeded in securing a general and warm popularity." The *Journal* attributed this warm reception to the affability, intelligence, and public-spirited character of President Birch and his associates.

The elegant headquarters of the new concern were in the Orleans Hotel, which stood on Second Street, between J and K streets, in Sacramento. It was a large, three-story structure, simple, dignified, and rather impressive. Above the front first-story windows, running the full width of the building, was an awning. At one end of this awning appeared in big letters the words: "Cal. Stage Co.," and into and out of the entrance below poured the bustling traveling public. To the right of the Orleans Hotel, as one faced the building, stood the spacious home of Adams and Company Express. Two buildings farther to the right were the offices of the competing Wells, Fargo and Company express and banking concern.

These made truly a transportation block. Out in front stood numerous coaches in readiness to depart for varying points, and throughout the day and night no less than thirty coaches arrived and departed. At times extra ones were placed on lines to meet special situations. Perhaps nowhere in America was staging being conducted on such a large scale; perhaps nowhere else could one single staging company then boast that its horses, coaches, and other properties were assessed at $1,000,000.

The spread of mining operations throughout the extreme northern part of California and the completion, in 1860, of an all-stage road from Sacramento to Portland, Oregon, made the staging operations active and important in that part of the state. At first the main road from Sacramento to Shasta and points radiating out from there was along the Sacramento River, through Colusa and Red Bluff. As far north as Colusa stages could connect with the steamers of the California Steam Navigation Company; but farther north travelers were dependent upon stages as the best mode of travel. To Red Bluff the road was fair, but north of this point it became increasingly rough and treacherous.

Another important stage artery by 1855 was the one leading northward from Sacramento, duplicating the one just described as far as Vernon, along the Feather River to Marysville and to Bidwell's Bar. Into it led numerous other branch roads which connected the great central valley with such thriving mining towns as Rough and Ready, Grass Valley, Nevada City, and Downieville. Beginning in the summer of 1852 the two major routes diverging at Vernon were rejoined far to the north when Hall and Crandall opened their new line between Marysville and 'Shasta City by way of Hamilton and Bidwell's Bar.

There followed considerable argumentation between Colusa and Marysville over which city could offer the quickest service to Shasta City. The Colusans considered their route a "natural" gateway to the northern mines, whereas travel "via Marysville will necessarily be forced."

To such a statement the proponents of the eastside route took great exception and argued that any disadvantages of their route could easily be offset by "Messrs. Hall & Crandall, the spirited proprietors of the San Jose mail line." Perhaps the argument was settled in Marysville's favor when, in 1859, the California Stage Company chose the eastside route as the official one for its Sacramento-to-Portland operations. By then the roads had become greatly improved and, contended the *Sacramento Union*: "A person . . . . who has no desire to risk his life on the rough coast of Oregon, can take a quiet seat in a stage, pass through a most interesting section of the country, and reach Portland at his leisure. . . . . Such an event as the starting of a Daily Mail stage to Portland should be announced by the firing of cannon and other indications of enthusiasm."

Travelers in the environs of Stockton, also a gold-rush boom town, have left records very similar to those which pertain to the Sacramento region. On a trip between there and Sonora, also in 1851, Frank Marryat, another British traveler, seems to have endured the irritations of Sir Henry Huntley rather than to have experienced the exhilarations of J. D. Borthwick. Marryat likewise complained about his fellow-passengers, among them a Canadian woman "who traveled under the protection of an ill-looking dog," a "quarrelsome and bumptious" Yankee armed with a revolver, and two or three miners who "squirted their juice at passing objects on the road with astonishing accuracy."

Marryat's journal gives a vivid, although exaggerated, picture of the roadside inns, where travelers ate and horses were exchanged. The stereotyped bills of fare, according to Marryat, consisted "of a tough beefsteak, boiled potatoes, stewed beans, a nasty compound of dried apples, and a *jug of molasses.*" But to a hungry passenger this food must have been more than welcome, for he would "sit down at the summons of a bell . . . . and, with the point of his knife . . . . taste of the various condiments . . . . pile them on his plate, demolish them with relish, and depart on his way in peace."

A soberer account of a ride over the Stockton-Sonora route has been given by Hinton R. Helper, famed author of *The Impending Crisis.* Leaving Stockton early in the morning, as was the custom, Helper said the coach went "as fast as a dare-devil driver can make four horses" go. The stage passed over a "somewhat elevated plain," which, being "entirely destitute of trees and other vegetable products," presented a "most dreary and uninviting prospect."

About twelve o'clock the stage reached the Stanislaus River, where lunch was served and a fresh team was secured. With the approach to Sonora the terrain changed "from level plains to rugged slopes and woodlands," and the road, which had been "disagreeably dusty" but both smooth and straight, now became winding as it advanced over "rocky glades, hills and gullies," with the result that the passengers were "jarred and shaken without mercy."

Helper and his fellow-passengers reached Sonora between sundown and dark and went to a public house for supper and lodging. Helper's account of Sonora's best hostelry is far from pleasant:

"The best hotel in the place is a one-story structure, built of unhewn saplings, covered with canvas and floored with dirt. It consists of one undivided room, in which the tables, berths and benches are all arranged. Here we sleep, eat and drink. Four or five tiers of berths or bunks, one directly above another, are built against the walls of the cabin. . . . . The bedding is composed of a small straw mattress about two feet wide, an uncased pillow . . . . and a single blanket."

The most treacherous roads appear to have been those narrow, winding, and precipitous mountain defiles of the upper Feather River and tributaries of that stream. It was over such a road that Dame Shirley traveled one September day in 1851. She wrote:

"I seated myself in the most excruciating springless wagon that it was ever my lot to be victimized in, and commenced my journey in earnest. I was the only passenger. For thirty miles the road passed through as beautiful a country as I had ever seen. Dotted here and there with the California oak, it reminded me of the peaceful apple orchards and smiling river meadows of dear old New England. As a frame to the graceful picture, on one side rose the Buttes, that group of hills so piquant and saucy; on the other, tossing to Heaven the everlasting whiteness of their snow-wreathed foreheads, stood, sublime in their very monotony, the glorious Sierra Nevada."

Dame Shirley remarks that the road ceased to be smooth and became stony and hilly in the mountainous region near Bidwell's Bar. "For more than a mile we drove along the edge of a precipice, and so near that it seemed to me, should the horses deviate a hair's breadth from their usual track, we must be dashed to eternity."

Stagecoach travel was never entirely safe, even on the smoothest roads. Quite apart from holdups, the newspapers of the day tell only too frequently of disastrous accidents attending routine travel. The causes of these accidents were numerous and varied. A common cause was a sudden lurch of the coach upon sinking deeply into a rut or hole, thereby tossing the driver to the ground behind the horses and in front of the heavy wheels of the coach. In such manner did the venerable and veteran stageman, J. B. ("Bob") Crandall, lose his life on November 25, 1872. The accident occurred eight miles from San Francisco and very near his own home. As Crandall fell behind his rear team, he was kicked by one of the horses and tossed on his head against the pole, or

tongue, with such violence that his skull was fractured. Not realizing the seriousness of the injury, the indomitable Crandall stag-
gered to his feet, assured himself of the safety of his one passenger,
took care of the mail and baggage, and then went to his home. He
told his family that he felt a "little hurt," lay down on his bed,
and died three hours later.

Recklessness of drivers, particularly new ones, was frequently
responsible for accidents, and the case of driver A. D. Spaulding
will serve as an illustration. Heavy rains caused Whisky Creek
to rise above the bridge. When Spaulding's stage approached the
creek at dusk, the inhabitants of Whiskytown advised against
attempting a crossing. Spaulding disregarded the admonitions,
and no sooner had the lead team struck water than it was lifted
and began going downstream, carrying rear team, coach, occupants, and all over some falls in the creek. The driver and his two
passengers, one of whom rescued the express box, managed to
reach shore. Two of the horses drowned; the other two were
found alive far downstream on the following day. Not long after
this, Spaulding was involved in another accident in which eight
or nine passengers were seriously hurt, one a soldier who lost an
arm. Henry W. Corbett of Portland, then the proprietor of the
line, paid the soldier $5,000 in cash and all his medical expenses.

Often, though, Lady Luck was on the box beside the driver,
as on one nice June morning in 1860 when driver Daniel Robbins
was ascending Goodyear's Bar Hill. Suddenly "the bank under
the outer wheel gave way, precipitating the coach a distance of
about one hundred feet below." We are told that for twenty feet
of this distance the stage fell perpendicularly and for the rest it
rolled. At the time of the accident there were three passengers
in the coach; and, "strange to say, only one of them was hurt, and
he only slightly bruised. "

The building of a stage station was an evolutionary process.
Both a barn and a granary must be built, places and food for the
horses and mules having to be provided at about ten-mile intervals. Human beings, on the other hand, could go hungry and un-
sheltered if necessary. Only if business seemed to warrant it did
the station man expand it into the tavern business.

Inconveniences incidental to stagecoach travel were numerous.
Something has already been said about taverns and their offer-

ings in the way of food and lodging. Even as late as 1860 a traveler, who wrote as "Roadster," bemoaned the fact that travel then still had the flavor of '49. "Spanish beef is served up regularly, and for dessert we have old fashioned pies made of dried peaches —even the bouquet of whisky flavors of the early times."

While this critic refers specifically to Yreka, he says that his remarks "will apply generally to keepers of public houses on all stage routes in California." He says California was then eight or nine years behind the times, because the day of dried-fruit pies with "paste board" crust, bedless bunks, and yellow soap was a thing of the past in other parts of the United States. He pointed out that stage proprietors are better known than innkeepers, and for this reason the stagemen get the blame for the poor fare.

Somewhere along the line tired and half-starved passengers would arrive at a hotel where meals were served. And what did they get to eat? "Half-cooked beans, heavy bread, stale butter, and bread pudding," says Roadster.

He concludes with the remarks that in traveling over most of California's stage roads, although not over-delicate in his own tastes and not a growler, he has had his "ears pained many times with the griefs of others." In many places he found taverns falling into decay and grass growing before the door, for the reason that new ones had emerged near by and had captured the trade.

And what a joy a good modern tavern would be! "Instead of wading through mud and slush to find a dirty wash basin, dirtier towels and 'yaller' soap, or no soap at all, he finds a sheltered washroom, with all the appoint[ment]s of a well-ordered hotel; . . . . is greeted by a tidy woman, who welcomes him to a chair at her table. The table covering and crockery are spotless white; a clean knife, fork and spoon are ready to his hand; everything is served up in good home style, and scrupulously neat and clean."

Such were some of the recorded experiences and impressions of travelers of the gold-rush days. Stagecoach travel had its charms and delights, but for many people it was exhausting, dirty, and even frightening. For those who had iron constitutions, for those who loved scenery, horses, and fellow human beings, for those who did not object to being either tossed unceremoniously on the laps of others or being on the receiving end, stagecoach riding could be a happy experience.

Chapter 3

THE COMING OF EXPRESS

AMN THE POSTMASTER! WHY CAN'T we git our mail? Hain't had a letter up here since I come."

"No use blaming the Postmaster, Chris, the whole bloomin' system's rotten. Them fellers back in Washington can't keep pace with Californy. Why, Lord a'mighty, they only giv' us one post office for the whole durn ter'tory."

"Wall, it's 'bout time they git agoin'!"

"You should complain!" chimed in a long-bearded gentleman who overheard this conversation. "Why, last week I stood in line all night long—in rain and mud—only to have that clerk at the window there say the next morning: 'There is nothing here for you.'"

Such was the confusion and delay at the San Francisco Post Office, a small frame building at the corner of Pike and Clay streets, during the spring months of 1849. The lines often extended down Clay Street as far as the Plaza, along Pike Street and even across Sacramento Street, where the tent population lived.

In order to avoid such long delays, those who could afford to do so employed and paid "handsomely" for substitutes who would hold a place in the line.

Not until the summer of 1849 were numerous post offices established, and at no time during the Gold Rush did the United States postal system function very satisfactorily. Before the authorities could take cognizance of some new mining camp, likely as not the town's population had gone to some new strike. Nothing seemed stationary in California, least of all mining camps and

28

towns. Such is the history of Foster's Bar, Shaw's Flat, Coon Hollow, Skunk Gulch, Rat Trap Slide, Yankee Jim's, Nigger Hill, Chinese Camp, Dixie Valley, Methodist Creek, and scores of other places with picturesque names which first boomed and then suddenly bcame dead, empty "ghost" towns. In the face of this situation the best the postal authorities felt they could do was to set up offices in towns which to them seemed relatively permanent. Such places as Sacramento, Stockton, and Marysville were among the earliest to be established.

But even with the extension of the postal system the service remained abominable. Said Sacramento's *Placer Times,* August 25, 1849: "The 'Regular Mail' is a regular humbug, is stuck in the mud half of the time, and might as well be the other half." And the *California Farmer* came out with: "There is no telling what number of letters miscarry, or are stolen, through the neglect or crime of Postmasters of this State." The post offices, this newspaper went on to say, "are generally kept in *doggeries* . . . . and, when the mail arrives, it is opened publicly, [and] . . . . everybody has access."

Here then was a problem crying out for a solution, and it was not long before ingenious Westerners found at least a way around this troubled spot.

It happened this way. One sunny day, in the early summer of 1849, a man named Alexander H. Todd suddenly appeared in the bustling mining town of Jacksonville. He came with an idea and a plan. Around him soon gathered a group of homesick, letter-hungry miners, to whom Todd made a proposition. For one dollar apiece he would record the names of the miners. Then, as their authorized agent, he would go back to San Francisco, collect his clients' letters, and deliver them in person at the mines. For this service Todd would ask for an ounce of gold dust per letter. But who wouldn't gladly pay an ounce of "dust" for news from a best girl, a wife, or a friend? To the grizzled miners this seemed cheap and "mighty accommodatin' " to say the least.

"And, Todd, while you're at it, why not deposit some of this here dust in one o' them new banks down in Frisco?" This Todd would do gladly—for another reasonable fee of five per cent.

"And, Mister Todd," inquired another, "if you're not gonna go fer an hour or so, would sure like to write a letter to my wife and have you mail it down yonder. Will ya do that?" For such a favor this engaging entrepreneur also collected a small fee.

A new business had arrived in the West, and to it belongs the name "express."

To be sure, Todd was not the originator of express. From ancient times on, errands had been run for a consideration. On the other hand, express as a regular business enterprise was rather new. It had begun fifteen years before as a bank-messenger service on the Boston and Providence Railroad. In California, however, Todd was, by his own admission at least, the first regular expressman. Perhaps, though, Charles Kimball should have this distinction, for Kimball and Company's Express operating out of Sacramento was the first to advertise this business in the newspapers.

In a written statement to the historian, H. H. Bancroft, Todd told how welcome his services were. He related that within a very short time he had over 2,000 names on his "express list." Todd and Company's Express operated until 1851. Its permanent headquarters were at Stockton, where it was the only express company for a time. The company improved its services by running daily express between the mining camps and San Francisco, as well as by making business connections with other companies operating outside of its territory, in order to take care of the increased activities in mining in the region east of Stockton. "Our express business extended rapidly from the first," Todd wrote; ". . . . we were taking every camp from Stockton to Jacksonville, and from Jacksonville to the Gold Creeks. . . . . It was a very common thing for me to start out from Stockton with two horses, loaded down with gold dust." Todd declares that for several months his business earned $1,000 a day.

In 1852 this pioneer business was absorbed by a powerful competitor, the Adams and Company Express; but, throughout the gold-rush period, the highly respected Todd continued his association with express and allied businesses.

It did not take a business genius to figure out that in California the express business promised lucrative returns for a relatively modest investment of capital. At first men such as Todd and Kimball provided their own horses and wagons (and in the more remote mountain regions, pack mules), but before long it was found to be more economical for them to make arrangements with the ever-increasing number of stagecoach and steamboat operators for handling express matter. Thus, by October 1849, for example, the express company advertisements would read as follows:

"Kimball and Co.'s Express to San Francisco by steamer . . . . ;" and again: "Weld & Co.'s Express . . . . connects at this point [Sacramento] with Mr. Birch's Express and Stage Line, which leaves here every morning for Mormon Island and Sutter's Mill."

In some instances the stage operators were their own expressmen, but as a rule this was not so. The conveying of express goods required special handling, special confidence on the part of the public, and attention to details which the stagemen preferred to avoid. Aboard ship a special safe was installed to house the valuables, and a special express agent was usually on hand to supervise transit procedures. Wherever there was danger from hold-ups — and such danger always existed along lonely mountain roads—a special guard known as a "shotgun messenger" sat beside the driver to discourage would-be "agents." Thus the express business emerged and expanded as a separate enterprise that was, nevertheless, very closely related to steamboating and stagecoaching in California.

The growth of small express companies became so popular that by 1860 the number now known to have existed in the Golden State exceeded 260 and may very well have reached or surpassed 300. A count can be made from interesting hand-franked envelopes, each of which bore the name of the express company handling a particular letter. Names of companies may also be gleaned from newspaper advertisements. But in all likelihood there are many of these pioneer, pack-mule expressmen whose names are unfortunately lost to posterity.

By 1852 a pattern of operation had developed. By then individual expresses were operating in somewhat clearly defined geographical areas. In the Mother Lode country San Francisco, Sacramento, and Stockton were main entrepôts through which incoming and outgoing commodities were funneled. In the Mariposa, Tuolumne, and Calaveras area first the firm of Todd and later that of Reynolds and Company led the field. In and around Placerville the firm of Hunter and Company's Express was best known. Langton's Pioneer Express, managed by resourceful and

much-beloved Sam W. Langton, dominated the Downieville area.
F. D. Everts operated through the Feather River region, the
Whiting and Company Express in remote Quincy, and, lastly,
Cram, Rogers and Company in the extreme northern California
district consisting of the three large counties of Shasta, Trinity,
and Siskiyou. Each of these leading concerns had numerous competitors, and, as years passed, many shifts and reorganizations
occurred.

Because of this localization of express operations the exchange
of goods among the several regions was considerably retarded.
Except by comparison with the federal postal system, speed and
efficiency were not necessarily characteristic of early express service in California. Although commodities were usually carried on
horseback, until 1852, and even later, pack mules, dog teams, and
men on foot carried express.

The minor companies faced other handicaps besides lack of
efficiency. They could not afford to house their offices in fire- and
burglar-proof buildings such as those which the large consoli-
dated firms eventually constructed. Losses from fire and theft
were frequent. Todd was "burned out" nine times in the few
years he was in business, and, even though he "was almost ex-
empt from interference" on the road, was often robbed by his
helpers. Wrote Todd: "One of our confidential clerks in 1852
robbed us of $70,000 in Stockton, another of $50,000 in Mariposa, and another of $40,000 at Mokelumne Hill."

In spite of their shortcomings, the minor companies, or "one-
man" expresses, rendered a real service. Their most important
functions were, as has been noted, the delivery of mail and the
conveyance of gold dust; but it was not long before their service
included also the handling of small parcels of every description—
drafts, notes, and bills, and even the purchasing of goods such
as a new pair of trousers, a new pick and shovel, or a Colt's revolver for miners stranded on some distant bar.

Expressing appreciation for this new service, the *Alta California* said on July 27, 1850: "EXPRESS COMPANIES. We
scarcely know what we should do if it were not for the various
Express lines established, enabling us to hold communication with
the mines. With the present defective mail communication we
should scarcely ever be able to hear from the towns throughout

California, or the remote portions of the Placers, north and south. . . . . Their expenses are necessarily very heavy and it requires a liberal patronage to remunerate them."

The inadequacy of the government postal system meant prosperity for the express companies. "Business men now have to depend entirely on the expresses," one of them wrote in 1853. A year later, when the government renewed its efforts to enforce the use of its stamps on letters sent by express, the *Alta California* stated that Washington was simply taxing the express companies "for accommodating our people." The *California Chronicle* asserted that, "in this State, where it would be next to impossible to carry on business without the expresses, this command [to buy stamps] is not only burdensome, but tyrannical."

Alonzo Delano, the contemporary illustrator of life in California, who in 1850 went to the mines east of Sacramento, has left a vivid description of the work of the expressmen, an account which clearly shows the importance of these men in the early days of the Gold Rush. "At nearly every bar where there is a store," says Delano, "a letter memorandum is kept by some merchant, where the miners who desire to obtain their letters from the post-office in the valley can enter their names"; these are taken by the expressman "who makes it his business to get from the post-office all letters and papers directed to his subscribers, and deliver them to the individuals at their diggings. . . . . There is scarcely a gulch which he does not visit," added Delano, and his arrival at camp was looked upon as an event of considerable importance. " 'The Express has arrived!' Every pick and shovel is dropped, every pan is laid aside, every rocker is dropped with its half-washed dirt . . . . and they crowd around the store, with eager enquiries, 'have you got a letter for me?' " Concluding his sketch of these expressmen, he says: "Without him, the miner would be shut out from the world, and next to the trader, who furnishes the means of sustaining life, the Express man is of the most importance."

In commenting upon the progress made in the transportation business in California up to October 1851, the *Alta California* paid this tribute to the express companies: "Express lines have furthered the interests of our commercial classes, and become of indispensable service to the mining population; penetrating the most remote recesses of the mineral region, and intersecting the country, threading the rivers and streams to their head waters, and following the highways, the byway and the wilderness track, wherever the adventurer has pushed his explorations, and established among human wants that of facile communication with his neighbor and the busy world."

No better summary of the entire subject can be given than that in the *California Chronicle* for May 4, 1854:

"Scarcely had California ceased to be Mexican, when the Express system was established all over the country. In this land of gold, where fortunes were made or lost, in a day's time, ... it soon became a matter of vital necessity that Expresses should be started. Different parties took different districts under their charge, and supplied with the Express accommodation that was wished. The arrangements of the Government Post Office, proverbially slow and uncertain, were no bar in the way of the Express Companies. In fact, both the interior and the ocean mails only served, by their provoking delays, to call attention to the usefulness, to the great comparative speed and safety of the Expresses themselves."

The esteem in which these many express companies were held by Californians may in part be explained by the keen competition that arose within the business itself. We have already noted how within each district one or two concerns outsmarted their competitors and rose to a position of prominence and leadership. Not infrequently this system was achieved by either consolidation or purchase of hard-pressed rivals. As time went on, this trend toward consolidation and bigness continued at an accelerated pace.

So long as this competitive scramble remained a local, a purely California family struggle, then ingenuity, personality, and super-energy usually brought their own rewards. But when, as actually happened, "outside" capital and connections were tossed into the balance, the prize went to those Easterners with the fattest pocketbooks.

At length two remarkable concerns made their debut in California and in due time stole the show. The first of these was Adams and Company, the second Wells, Fargo and Company Express.

Alvin Adams was the founder of the firm which bears his

name. As head of his still youthful and growing enterprise Adams was nevertheless a veteran with nine years' experience behind him by the time Alexander Todd first offered his services to the miners of Jacksonville. Adams, moreover, was a shrewd, cautious, and thrifty Vermonter. In the Green Mountain state he had served his apprenticeship in catering to the public. At age sixteen Alvin had become a hotel clerk, soon afterward a grocer. Gradually he rose to the proud position of a produce merchant, successively in Woodstock (Vermont), Boston, and New York City. In each of these later undertakings he failed; but with each failure he gained wisdom, and ultimately he was to succeed.

It was in 1840 that the attention of Adams turned to the infant, yet promising, Eastern business of express. With a partner, P. B. Burke, young Adams invested his small savings (each contributed one hundred dollars) and together they organized the New York and Boston Express Company. Their method of doing businesss was very simple. The partners started by buying two season tickets on the New York and Boston Railroad. Adams would leave Boston one day with his bag of valuables for delivery in New York City, and Burke would leave New York City for Boston. On the following day each would go back to the other city.

After a few months of this routine, Burke withdrew; but Adams stuck it out. The next year, 1841, he expanded his business, as the volume of parcels grew. Soon his activities widened to include all New England; soon, too, the profits began rolling in. In fact, so successful did Adams and Company become that within twelve years after its founding this express firm was capitalized at $10,000,000 and Alvin Adams was the proud president of the organization.

This company became the first powerful and dominating influence in the light-parcels-carrying trade of California. When news of the gold discovery reached the officers of Adams and Company in the East, it is only natural that their thoughts should have turned toward the Golden Gate.

"Just think of it, gentlemen," Adams might have told his Board of Directors. "Every day that passes sees hundreds of people leaving our coastal cities for San Francisco. Every man who goes West will want to receive letters from home. Thousands will find gold which they will want sent East to the United States

Mint. Never before in my nine years in the express has such an opportunity for business expansion opened before us."

Then, turning to Daniel Haskell, Adams' appointed "resident partner" in California, he might also have asked this question:

"How soon can you get to San Francisco?"

What words actually passed between Haskell and President Adams we can only imagine. But Haskell lost no time in departing. He traveled the Isthmus route, and on October 31, 1849, he arrived in San Francisco. On November 8, only nine days after his arrival, the following announcement appeared in the *Alta California:*

"Adams & Co.'s Express for New York, Boston, and the principal towns in the New England States, Philadelphia, Baltimore, Washington, etc., etc., etc. Gold dust bought, also forwarded to any of the above places, and bills of exchange given in any amounts. Letter-bags made up and forwarded by a special messenger in each of the steamers. Office, for the present, in Sacramento street, over Collins, Cushman & Co.

"A. ADAMS, Boston,
"W. B. DINSMORE, N. York, } *Proprietors"*
"D. H. HASKELL, San Fr'sco,

From what had been a modest beginning, though with substantial backing, the California branch of the Adams concern rose to a position of power and prominence far exceeding any of its rivals, except one.

In California Haskell hastened to make connections with desirable Isthmian and local express concerns. Among the first of such connections in 1849 was Whitney and Ely's Express for transfer via Panama. During 1850 Hawley and Company announced themselves as exclusive agents for Adams in Sacramento. In this year Todd tied up with Adams, and in the year following, Freeman and Company and Hunter and Company did likewise.

By the opening of 1852 the Adams organization in California had not only become state-wide in scope but had introduced many new features which made it superior to any of its competitors. It had introduced a pony-express system to give some of the more important mining camps better access to San Francisco. The

Sonora from the north (from a contemporary lithograph)

A roadside inn and stagecoach of the 'fifties
(from a contemporary photograph)

ponies were much faster than the cumbersome express wagons, stages, and river steamers which had before conveyed gold dust, letters, and other shipments of express. Moreover, until the establishment of Wells, Fargo and Company in California in the summer of 1852, Adams and Company was the only firm to have a "special messenger" accompanying its semi-monthly treasure shipments between San Francisco and New York. This made the transportation of express across the Isthmus more rapid and gave greater protection against loss by robbery, theft, and fire. And, too, as previously stated, the Eastern network made possible the quick delivery of goods when they arrived in New York. Adams and Company was the only firm which had the right to send express on the mail trains running between New York and Philadelphia, "thereby insuring a sooner delivery at the mint than any other conveyance." The concern also developed a banking business in conjunction with its regular express business.

By 1853, Adams and Company was generally regarded as the leading business house in California. It handled more money, dealt with more people, and furnished more accommodations to industry and commerce than any other establishment.

In paying personal tribute to Adams, who visited California in 1853, the *San Francisco Sun* referred to him as one whose name was then famous throughout the whole world, although only a few years before "he drove his own express wagon, delivering the packages and other express matter." He was a man who, "knowing the true secret of success had indomitable perseverance, which knows no obstacles or abatement in its onward course, ... persevered, and now stands without rival in the express business in the world!"

By March 15, 1855, the company's assets in California totaled $1,863,775.42. Of this sum, $536,148.76 were in the form of loans to depositors, which shows the emphasis which was given to banking. Out of this huge total, $227,622.61 were on hand and in buildings; $25,000 were represented by horses, wagons, and fixtures; $334,846.11 were in gold dust; and the remainder was in bills receivable, private property of I. C. Woods, and that of other persons connected with the concern. Excess over liabilities totaled $223,487.17—a relatively small margin. But the volume of its business and the amount of capital involved placed Adams and

Company, up to 1855, among the first-rank business houses of California.

By the middle 'fifties the trend in the express field clearly paralleled that of steamboating and staging. No longer was it possible for the small pack-mule expresses that earlier had served isolated mining communities to compete on favorable terms with concerns organized and operating on a national basis. In the grim, competitive struggle during this heroic age of American free business enterprise, the "little fellow" lost out. The express business was heading inevitably toward consolidation, toward monopoly. In this capacity Wells, Fargo and Company was to play a major role.

Chapter 4

WELLS FARGO TRIUMPHANT

ENRY WELLS WAS BORN IN Thetford, Vermont, on December 12, 1805. He grew up to become a broad-shouldered, powerful-looking man. His face was described by one who knew him as having a "Romanesque contour, with a large Caesarian nose." He possessed a sharp, keen, yet kindly face—and Henry Wells was a kindly man. Wells was late in hitting upon his life work. His thirties saw him on the New York waterfront, where he was a steamboat operator in and out of this thriving metropolis. He did not remain with the boats long enough to have them "get into his system," and in 1841 he became interested in the new express business about which there must have been a great deal of talk in transportation circles. He went to Albany and there took employment with William F. Harnden, pioneer expressman. Wells tells us that he did not stay with Harnden very long, and before the close of 1841 he joined with George E. Pomeroy and Crawford Livingston in establishing an express line between Albany and Buffalo, New York.

Wells served as express messenger over his company's line. The work was hard—very hard. "At that time," he tells us, "there was no continuous line of railroads or stages over this route." Private conveyance had to supplant existing facilities, and four nights and three days was "the quickest attainable route of traveling." Wells worked diligently to be successful and states that often he spent eighteen out of twenty-one nights on the road. For over a year a carpetbag held all the express matter confided to him and it was some time before his receipts covered his traveling expenses. Not until the partners hit upon the idea of carrying fresh fruit, fish, lobsters, and oysters to help Buffaloans vary their menus did some profits accrue. Attention, too, was directed to the new concern when in 1842 it offered to carry letters at a rate far cheaper than that offered by the Post Office Department. This competition with the postal system, incidentally, began a protracted legal battle with the government.

It was in connection with express operations that Henry Wells became acquainted with an energetic and hard-working man named William George Fargo. Fargo was a native of Pompey, New York, having been born there on May 20, 1818, the first of a family of twelve children. Little did the good people of Pompey think that some day this Fargo child would become a national figure. Not until they saw him, a lad of thirteen, galloping on horseback over his forty-mile mail route did the home folks begin to appreciate in young William his many likeable and commendable qualities.

He was the type of person that frontier society admired—ambitious, frugal, and anxious to get ahead. He tried many jobs, and we see him successively as postman, grocer, freight agent on the new Auburn and Syracuse Railroad, and then, in 1843, as messenger for the express firm of which Wells was a partner. Fargo served in this capacity for two years, after which Wells accepted Fargo as a partner in a new express organization that would serve Chicago, Cincinnati, and St. Louis.

Thus began the partnership which, with many business shifts, was to endure for life and bring great fame and fortune to the names of Wells and Fargo.

Ever since the mad rush to the California diggings had begun, no person engaged in the express business could easily stand aloof from the prospects of making money. Wells, Fargo, and their associates were no exception. Business difficulties in the East, however, had not permitted these gentlemen to plunge into the California competition in 1849, and three years elapsed before they felt financially secure enough to do so. By then their competitor, Alvin Adams, was already strongly entrenched on the West Coast and, as Wells later recalled, it "demanded much courage and determination" to establish another company in the face of the "formidable opposition" offered by Adams and Company.

Such a move was nevertheless considered practical, and definite

plans for the formation of a new California express concern were
made. New York financiers were deeply interested in the project,
and with their substantial backing a new company was organized
on March 18, 1852.

The name given this new concern has outlived all others of
Gold Rush days. It was to be the Wells, Fargo and Company.
It was not long before Westerners, with their genius for shorten-
ing names, referred to the firm simply as "Wells Fargo" or, at
best, "Wells Fargo Express." And such popularity did the organization achieve that Wells Fargo soon became a household term.
Miners would write of sending their gold dust "by Wells Fargo."
People the country over would speak of sending letters, parcels,
and, in fact, everything from finger rings to a wife and child "by
Wells Fargo Express." There was not much that this organization would not and could not do in the name of public service.

But let us return to that important business meeting of stockholders in New York City where the details of organization were
being ironed out. Present, and prominently so, were the promoters, Wells, Fargo, and Johnston Livingston—the latter, a
successor to Crawford Livingston who died in 1847. Present, too,
were the men who held the bulging purses, especially the prominent
New York banker, Edwin B. Morgan. Fargo, acting as President
pro tem, called the meeting to order, and officers were chosen. No
surprise: Morgan was elected President; James McKay was
chosen Secretary and General Counsel; Livingston was elected
Chairman of the Executive Committee; and, along with these officers and four others, Wells and Fargo were made directors of the
Company. The new firm was officially named Wells, Fargo and
Company because the two men whose names the firm was to bear
were the chief promoters and the men already best known in the
express field. The concern was termed a joint stock company, and
it was registered under the general incorporation laws of New
York State. Its capitalization was given as $300,000.

The organization was now complete and attention was turned
to California. The results of this action came in May 1852, when
Samuel P. Carter, previously connected with the American Express Company, was charged with the specific duty of setting up
the forwarding branch of the business in the West Coast state. A
second appointee, Reuben W. Washburn, because of his ex-

perience as a banker, was instructed to establish the banking department of Wells, Fargo and Company in San Francisco. This procedure indicated that Wells, Fargo and Company, like its Adams and Company competitor, planned from the outset to broaden its services to include banking along with that of forwarding express. On May 20 everything was set, and on that date the first public announcement appeared in the *New York Times*.

"This company having completed its organisation . . . .," reads the announcement, "is now ready to undertake the general forwarding agency and commission business; the purchase and sale of gold dust, bullion, and specie, also packages, parcels and freight of all description in and between the City of New York and the City of San Francisco, and the principal cities and towns in California. . . . .

"They have established offices and faithful agents in all the principal cities and towns throughout the eastern, middle and western states, energetic and faithful messengers furnished with iron chests for the security of treasure and other valuable packages accompany each express upon all their lines as well as in California and in the Atlantic States."

Certain facts, then, are evident. Wells, Fargo and Company, was, unlike the scores of minor California expresses, Eastern in origin. It was organized chiefly through the efforts of Henry Wells, William A. Fargo, Johnston Livingston, and their immediate associates in Eastern express matters, its center of operations being western New York State. These men and New York City capitalists furnished the capital to back the concern. It is, however, clear that its chief field of operations was to be, and certainly did become, California.

The California press gave the new Wells, Fargo and Company a warm send-off, as illustrated by the *San Francisco Herald,* on July 2, 1852: "A glance at the list of directors will satisfy anyone of the unlimited confidence which may be reposed in the establishment."

Washburn, who reached San Francisco two weeks later than Carter, arrived on the steamer *Tennessee* on July 11, bringing with him sixty-five packages, which were probably the first shipment of express by Wells, Fargo and Company between the Atlantic and the Pacific states. From July 11 on, the San Francisco office received regular semi-monthly express shipments from the East; and, from July 30 on, it sent gold dust and other parcels out of San Francisco with equal regularity. Within a month the Western agents of Wells, Fargo and Company were able to give adequate service to the California miners.

The next problem after the organization of the business was to determine the exact relationship between the express and the banking departments. During the first year Carter and Washburn shared the same building and advertised jointly; but there is every indication that the two departments were separated within the next two years. Separate records were kept; and, in 1855, when the bank was temporarily closed the express department continued to operate with its customary regularity.

The problems which Wells, Fargo and Company faced were comparable to those faced by Adams and Company in 1849. The success or failure of the concern was largely dependent upon the extent to which it could secure business in San Francisco's hinterland. Carter and Washburn directed their efforts toward the establishment of a state-wide organization during the summer of 1852. In October their work was completed. The *Register of First-Class Business Houses in San Francisco,* published that month, gives a fair estimate of the scope and character of the enterprise. This gives sufficient evidence that by October 1852 the Wells, Fargo and Company directors had been selected, its agents had become established in California, and its arrangements with the Pacific Mail Steamship Company, Hunter and Company, and Todd and Company for the transportation of its express parcels had been completed.

In November 1852, Wells, Fargo and Company purchased Gregory and Company's Express, effecting the first of numerous similar transactions made within the state of California. The acquisition of Gregory and Company's Express not only eliminated the competitor in the inter-coastal business but, for the first time, put Wells, Fargo and Company in control of an inland express line already doing a good business between San Francisco, Sacramento, and Stockton.

Only one of the frequent changes in the Board of Directors and other offices during the year 1853 directly affected California. Colonel William I. Pardee replaced Carter as manager of the Express Department in San Francisco, and became a member of the Board of Directors. After Pardee's arrival at San Francisco on July 7, 1853, several acquisitions were made by the Company, the first of which was the purchase of the Todd and Company Express on September 1, 1853.

With reference to this important purchase Wells, Fargo and Company made this public statement:

"Mr. Todd having disposed of his interest in the Southern Express to us, we shall run a Daily Express to and from

"San Francisco;	Columbia;
"Stockton;	Murphy's Flat;
"Sonora;	Moquelumne Hill.

"Connecting with a Daily Express at Stockton for Ophir and Mariposa.

"A Special Messenger is sent from San Francisco to Columbia.

"WELLS, FARGO & Co.,
"114 Montgomery St."

On January 17, 1854, the Board of Directors voted to increase the "working capital for California" to $150,000; and, with this amount at his disposal, Colonel Pardee made at least three important deals in 1854. The Wells, Fargo and Company express system was extended southward to include Los Angeles; arrangements were made with the newly established California Stage Company for handling Wells Fargo matter; and Hunter and Company Express, which operated in Eldorado and Placer counties, was purchased in July 1854.

The purchase of Hunter and Company Express enabled Wells Fargo to achieve its goal at last—ownership of a network of express lines covering every section of California. By three major moves—the purchase of Gregory and Company, of Todd and Company, and of Hunter and Company—this had been accomplished. By 1854 the company had twenty-four offices, most of which were in the Golden State; moreover, their San Francisco office building was greatly enlarged, and "for commodious apportionment and elegance of finish" it had, according to the *California Farmer,* "few superiors in the United States."

At last Wells, Fargo and Company felt strong enough and con-

Waiting in line for mail at San Francisco postoffice, corner of Pike and
Clay streets, in early Gold Rush days

Placerville in the 'fifties
(from a contemporary lithograph)

WILLIAM G. FARGO

HENRY WELLS

Wells, Fargo and Company's headquarters
in San Francisco, 1855

Sacramento from the waterfront during the middle 'fifties

fident enough to lock horns with its chief rival. Up until 1854 the Adams firm had enjoyed an advantage gained by time and resources. Now, with her connections established throughout the state, the Wells Fargo organization strove desperately to make a bid for leadership.

In the cutthroat competition that ensued, express rates between New York and San Francisco fell; so, too, did the time required for transit via the Isthmus route. Soon the press and public generally began sensing the treat—for such it was—that was in store for them.

One test of efficiency came when on December 28, 1853, a steamer arrived at San Francisco bearing an important Presidential message. This intelligence was to be conveyed to Portland, and important news of such a nature was usually forwarded by pony express instead of by stagecoach. Special pony-express riders would go in relays, and the companies throve on the free advertisement given them by a friendly press. On this occasion there ensued a race between the two great rivals. Each wanted to be the first to arrive in Portland with the news, for as yet there was no telegraphic connection with Oregon. Adams had an important hook-up in the northern part of this route with Cram, Rogers and Company; Wells Fargo had a similar connection with the Rhodes and Whitney Express.

So the race was on. At Marysville the Wells Fargo rider was in the lead. Somewhere between Marysville and Tehama the Adams man galloped ahead of his adversary. At Tehama the width of the Sacramento River was all that separated the riders, but this advantage still went to the Adams man. What happened from Tehama onward was told later by William S. Lowden, one of the riders for Adams:

"Here my race commenced. I sprang into the saddle with the bags, which weighed 54 pounds. I changed horses nineteen times between Tehama and Shasta, touching the ground but once. This was at the Prairie House, where Tom Flynn, the man in charge of my horse, was actively engaged in a fight with the keeper of Wells, Fargo's horse and had let mine get loose. I rode my tired horse a little past where the fight was going on, sprang to the ground, caught the fresh horse by the tail as he was running away from me and went into the saddle over his rump at a single bound. Turning to the horse I had just left with the express bags, I pulled them over on my fresh horse and renewed the race. I lost about one minute here.

"All other changes I made while the horses were running, the keeper leading the horse I was to ride and riding his extra horse. I would make myself heard with a whistle about half a mile before reaching the change, which gave ample time to tighten the cinch and start the fresh horse on the road. When I reached him, the keeper would have my horse in a lively gallop, and I sprang from the one to the other. . . . .

"I reached Shasta, sixty miles, in two hours and thirty-seven minutes. This was to end my ride, but the agent for Adams & Co. informed me that the man who had been engaged to make the side ride to Weaverville, one of the conditions of the race, was unable to do so, and I volunteered to take his place. About two minutes' time was required in dividing the express matter. I took the Weaverville portion, and Jack Horsley the Portland. I had nine changes of horses between Shasta and Weaverville (the last five being owned by me and hired by Adams for the race), and reached the latter place in five hours and thirteen minutes from the time I left Tehama. From Shasta to Weaverville was run after dark, with a light snow falling, but when I reached the mountains and had my favorite horses to ride—Wild Cat, Comanche, Greyhound, Pompey and Jack—snow did not make much difference in speed. . . . .

"I was so far ahead of Wells, Fargo's messenger at Shasta that they stopped the race there, as far as that company was concerned. It was well they did so, for Jack Horsley made a splendid ride from Shasta to Yreka, having covered half that distance when Wells, Fargo & Company's messenger reached Shasta. My stock and help for this race cost Adams & Company about $2,000."

If Wells Fargo men could not outride the Adams men, they could at least outrustle them. On December 15, 1854, the record shows that for the first time the Wells, Fargo and Company office handled more parcels than its rival. It scored 278, as against 240 for Adams.

Quite apart from its fight with Adams, the firm of Wells, Fargo and Company had become, by 1855, an organization closely identified with the welfare of the state. "The daily increasing business which crowns their efforts," remarked the *California Farmer* on January 25, 1855, "is the surest evidence of the faithfulness and dispatch with which all business matters are transacted, and of their influence, prosperity and popularity." The same article made it clear that by 1855 the influence of this firm had already extended beyond the realm of express, for the aggregate wealth of the banking department would have to be computed in millions of dollars. A good volume of business and strong public support were the foundations of this firm.

Anyway, the real and final test was not far off. During 1854 there were frequent signals of an impending general financial depression, and what counted was the ability to face a crisis. With each passing month, Wells, Fargo and Company continued to expand; but it did so cautiously, not recklessly. When a financial statement of this firm was published in February 1855, it showed assets amounting to $743,499.58 and liabilities of only $354,394.35. Balance to the credit of the house was $389,105.23. This statement gave evidence of sound finance. That Wells, Fargo and Company did operate on a highly solvent basis, and that the opposite was true in the case of its chief competitor, is well borne out by events.

On Friday, February 23, 1855, the Adams and Company Bank did not open its doors; the firm had failed. The results of this day were so momentous and tragic to the people of California that it has since been referred to as "Black Friday," a day of great misfortune.

The immediate causes of the failure of Adams and Company may be briefly told. On February 18, five days earlier, the steamer *Oregon* had arrived in San Francisco with the unwelcome news that the Page and Bacon Company of St. Louis, parent bank of Page, Bacon and Company of California, had suspended business. The St. Louis house had invested heavily in the Ohio & Mississippi Railroad (then building between Cincinnati and St. Louis), and when the latter concern faltered, the Page and Bacon Company was forced to close its doors. This news foreboded a similar fate for the California branch, for the latter company had not long before shipped $1,000,000 to the ill-fated St. Louis concern and, with its gold supply badly depleted, it was in no position to cope with an emergency.

The inevitable happened. Hardly had the *Oregon* docked when a report was circulated that Page, Bacon and Company of San Francisco was about to fail. The rumor was followed by a run on its bank, and California appeared definitely headed for a general financial panic. Newspapers, as is their custom, admonished the people that there was no need to be frightened. The *California Chronicle,* for instance, asserted that the firm was fully able to pay all of its obligations and expressed the belief that the vaults of the company contained $1,200,000. But all attempts to quiet fears were of no avail, and on February 22 the following public announcement was made: "We must suspend. . . . . We cannot raise coin on our bills. The coin is not in the country."

The intense excitement which pervaded San Francisco as a result of this announcement spread to other parts of the state. On February 22 Montgomery Street in San Francisco was filled with people standing in knots. The banks that remained open were besieged with men and women scrambling to the counters.

The situation in Sacramento was even more critical. Almost all the banks there closed on this date, after giving the following notice to the public: "We, the undersigned Bankers, hereby give notice, that we will not receive Checks on others in payment on Notes or Acceptances, nor will we certify Checks on ourselves"—signed "Adams and Company," "Page, Bacon and Company," "Wells, Fargo and Company, *et al.*" The news of the closing of the banks in Sacramento created such a stir, according to word received by the *Chronicle,* that many proposed to break down the doors and help themselves to the cash. "Never in the history of our young city," bemoaned the *Sacramento Union,* "have its merchants and business men passed a day of such anxiety, doubt and agitation. Business came nearly to a standstill, and men seemed almost paralyzed by the force and suddenness of the shock."

It is important to note here how the situation affected Adams and Company. Their bank remained open in San Francisco on February 22, but during the day more than $200,000 was withdrawn from accounts, while not more than $10,000 was placed on deposit. It became quite evident to the officers of the firm that under such circumstances their business could not long maintain itself. It was therefore decided at a meeting held on the evening of the 22nd that further payment—and this included all branch offices—was to be suspended. In accordance with this decision, I. C. Woods, president of the company, made the following public declaration on February 23, 1855:

"The undersigned, resident partner of Adams & Co. of California, in view of their suspension of payment this day, deems it his duty to present . . . . a brief statement of the causes that have led to this calamity. . . . .

"It is well known that the demand of gold for shipment has for many months far exceeded the supply of dust from the mines; to meet this deficiency, coin has been withdrawn from the circulation of the country at about the rate of one million dollars per month, leaving scarcely sufficient for the most ordinary wants of business, and producing an unparalleled and increasing pressure."

The public, upon receiving the news that Adams and Company had failed, became intensely excited. Public resentment became even more bitter than it had been toward Page, Bacon and Company. People suspected, perhaps rightly, that they had been defrauded. The belief prevailed that the company possessed a large gold reserve, and that it should at least have met, as Page, Bacon and Company had done before it, the demands for payment until this reserve was gone.

The gloom which had hung over San Francisco and Sacramento on the 22nd turned to anger on the 23rd, and again had its repercussions in the outlying parts of the state. From Grass Valley came the report that "the excitement produced by the announcement . . . . of the suspension of Adams and Company was inconceivably violent. . . . . A fire, threatening the total destruction of the town would not have caused a consternation so fearful and so deep." When the news reached Placerville, crowds collected around the bank and discussed their chances of recovering their deposits. The same thing happened in Auburn. A dispatch from that town stated that an armed crowd compelled the bank to reopen its safe and distribute its money among the depositors.

Equally disturbed were the citizens of Sonora, who, according to the *Chronicle*, "decided to make a forcible entry into the vault containing the treasure, which for several days previously had been under the sheriff's charge. A mob then broke into the vault, overpowering the Sheriff, and his assistants." Possession having thus been secured of the gold, tellers were appointed to pay it out, "who did so as fast as cheques could be presented."

In Nevada City, on the contrary, news of the suspension of business was received without much demonstration; but in Coloma, Diamond Springs, and Mormon Island, "a deep feeling" prevailed, says the *Sacramento Union,* "on account of the privations of the banking privilege."

It had originally been the hope of the officers of Adams and Company somehow to salvage its express business from the wreck. It advertised to that effect in the *Chronicle* for February 24: "The different Expresses of Adams & Co. for the Northern and Southern mines will leave today as usual. . . . . There will be no change or cessation in the Express business of this company."

The public, irate though it was over the suspension of banking operations, shared in the wish that the express department might continue as it had done since 1849. The *Sacramento Union* made an emotional appeal to its readers, urging that in the "day of their trial and tribulation" the people of California should realize that Adams and Company Express had been a real public benefactor. "Whatever may be the condition of Adams and Company at the present time," continued the *Union,* "it should be remembered in the mines, that they are the pioneer Expressmen in the State; their lines have penetrated to almost every mining camp in the State; they have not only conveyed letters and papers, but they sent coin into the interior by the hundreds of thousands and bought gold dust at liberal prices."

Despite the favorable popular feeling toward the express branch, it soon became apparent that it was to share the fate of the Adams and Company Bank; the two departments were too intimately related for the condition of one not to affect that of the other. On February 27, following three days of public demonstrations against the bank, it became apparent to the directors of Adams and Company that their firm could never re-establish itself in public esteem in California and that it would be necessary for the president, I. C. Woods, to file a petition of insolvency in the Fourth District Court. The petition was filed on February 28, and thus came to an inglorious end the express, as well as the banking, department of Adams and Company.

In the investigations that followed it was shown that not only had the Adams concern been reckless in the conduct of its business in California but irregularities, too numerous to mention here, had been committed. One statement by the courageous and outspoken James King of William, editor of the *San Francisco Bulletin,* will suffice: "That there has been cheating and swindling, and lying going on about the Adams and Company, we are as confident as that there was an eclipse of the moon last night."

Unlike the Adams house in 1855, Wells Fargo was controlled from New York City; and since the failure of the Page and Bacon Company of St. Louis was partly the result of the manipulations of a Wall Street firm, the directors of Wells, Fargo and Company were probably forewarned about what was to occur in California.

In any event, an interesting sequence of events took place in the East prior to the outbreak of the panic. On January 12, 1855, the drafts of the Page and Bacon Company (St. Louis) on Duncan, Sherman and Company (New York) were protested for nonpayment. This was known in New York, and may have precipitated a meeting of the Board of Directors of Wells, Fargo and Company held three days later. The Board, doubtless seeing the handwriting on the wall—the effect of a failure of the Page and Bacon Company on the San Francisco house of Page, Bacon and Company—sent special instructions to W. I. Pardee, its manager in California. And again on February 16, long before the news of the panic reached New York City, the directors met once more and "authorized the employment of a man," according to the minutes, "to go to California with full power to act for the Board."

Although neither the special instructions to Pardee nor the personal representative of the Board could have reached San Francisco before the panic had hit California and forced both Page, Bacon and Company and Adams and Company to the wall, there is some indication that the New York connection of Wells, Fargo and Company was increasingly important during the months of crisis.

The panic affected Wells, Fargo and Company very differently from the Adams concern. Wells Fargo banks, everywhere except in Sacramento, remained open on February 22, and the express business seems to have continued in full operation. But since they did not know how long the gold reserve could last, the

San Francisco bank was closed on the 23d with this announcement on its doors:

"To our Depositors—We have deemed it prudent for the protection of your interests as well as ours, to close our doors today. We shall make such a statement of our affairs and abundant ability to pay as we trust will satisfy all.

"WELLS FARGO and Co.

"San Francisco, Feb. 23, 1855."

Henry M. Naglee was immediately appointed temporary receiver for the firm, and on the following day, February 24, he made this statement regarding the status of the company:

"Wells Fargo & Co. have completed a balance of their accounts this day, and find to the credit of their house above every liability $389,106.23, and only ask of their friends a few days to convert some of their assets to resume payment.

WELLS FARGO & Co.

"Saturday, 10 p.m."

This encouraging declaration and other signs of the strength of the firm were soon to restore full confidence. Nearly all the offices in the interior were able to stand the runs made upon them and so remained open. And the Sacramento branch, which had been the first to close, was also the first to reopen, which assured Wells Fargo, in the words of the *Union,* of the "full confidence of the community."

The crisis was apparently over by February 26, and on the following day the San Francisco bank again resumed business, with the announcement from its receiver that the firm had "sufficient cash to meet all their cash liabilities, and sufficient assets to meet all their other liabilities, and leave a surplus in favor of the house of $103,473." The company had weathered the storm, and had "won . . . . an enviable fame." Like gold "seven times purified," the *California Farmer* stated, it comes "from the fiery ordeal with increased lustre," and sends "abroad a name and fame that will endure."

Since Wells, Fargo and Company became the outstanding express business in California after the panic of 1855, certain changes in its organization had to be made. The Board of Directors sent T. M. Janes, general treasurer for the firm, to California to replace Pardee as general agent. And on May 14, 1855, the Board increased the capital stock of the company from $500,000 to $600,000.

The first change proved to be temporary, for in October Louis McLane was appointed by Janes to take charge of the company's business in California. McLane was a retired United States naval officer and a resident of San Francisco. His appointment was fortunate in that he remained with the firm for a number of years, and under McLane's management the express business thrived as it never had before. He brought to his work, as one newspaper remarked, "a fresh and unusually vigorous spirit of enterprise and improvement."

Most important of the changes introduced by McLane in California was the introduction of government-stamped envelopes for letters with the franks of the company stamped on them. These became known as "franked" envelopes, and their sale to and use by the public represented prepayment of postage charges in place of the former system of handling mail on a collect basis.

This system, though not entirely new, was highly successful for Wells, Fargo and Company in California. The first month the system was tried receipts reached $400. Before the close of 1855 the sale of "franked" envelopes reached $10,676; and before the end of the decade the net income from the sale of the envelopes was $15,000 per month. Other changes made by McLane included the extension of the pony express system, investment in both local and transcontinental stage companies, an extension of lines, and an increase in the number of express offices in the state as rapidly as was necessary.

By the end of 1855 there were forty-two Wells Fargo express offices in the state, and by the close of the decade this number had more than tripled. Moreover, by 1860 the company had expanded throughout the whole of the Pacific Northwest, and such widespread service helped to knit that section more closely than ever before with California.

Chapter 5

KNIGHTS OF THE LASH

OT EVERYONE COULD MANAGE a stagecoach. A stage driver was a skilled operator, and was treated accordingly. Time was, as one old pioneer recalled, "when the man who held the ribbons over a six-horse team on the summit of the Sierra and in the cañons of the Coast and Cascade ranges was more highly esteemed than the millionaire or the statesman" who rode beside him.

"The average stage driver," wrote the historian Bancroft, was by no means the "least original and fantastic" of the conglomeration of humanity in California. Above all, he was the "lord in his way, the captain of his craft, the fear of timid passengers, the admiration of the stable-boys, and the trusty agent of his employer."

A knight, jehu, or whip (for by such names was he called) was, moreover, swaggering in his conduct, rather rough in his manner of speech, but, strange as it seems, usually very accommodating to his passengers—especially to the ladies. A driver ordinarily had the bare rudiments of an education and was celebrated for his pronounced, though probably not profound, views on all problems of state, religion, business, and love. Above all, he was expected to be sober and dependable.

Brigadier General James F. Rusling, who in his long travels learned to know the stage drivers well, had this to say of them:

"Off the box they were loquacious enough, but when mounted with four or six in hand, they either think it unprofessional to talk, or else were absorbed too much in their business. They each had fifty or sixty miles to make, up one day and back the next, and to the people along the route they were important personages. As bearers of the United States mail they felt themselves kings of the road and were seldom loath to show it. 'Clar the road! Git out of the way thar with your bull teams!' was a frequent salutation."

J. Ross Browne, another famous Western observer, did not share the general view that drivers were friendly and accommodating, although he liked certain individual ones. "Why stage-drivers, who are paid a liberal stipend per month for putting passengers over the public highways, should be so vindictively hostile to the travelling community surpasses my comprehension," he wrote.

As a rule, the passengers, and Browne among them, really idolized most drivers. The majority of men desired an outside seat when the weather was good, and, as we have seen, the prize seat of all was on the box with the driver. This was one place that was reserved. It was not gotten by being the first to hop up on the left front wheel rim and into the box. For, as Browne phrased it, "whether you be a Minister plenipotentiary or a member of the Common Council he [the driver] will exercise the right pertaining to his craft—order you down, and then enjoy your discomfiture for a distance of ten miles."

In seeking permission to sit in the driver's seat one proceeded very much in the manner of securing an appointment to a high office. One would go to the source of authority—above the driver himself—to the superintendent and even to the president of the company.

Drivers were able organizers and usually got people, together with their luggage, loaded into their coaches with great dispatch. Into the space in front of the station would come the driver with his stage. Toward it would hurry the crowd of passengers— ladies in their customary traveling crinoline coats, serious-looking business men, "John Chinaman" with pigtail dangling down his back. Then, as Browne reports:

"This way, gents!" the jehu would shout. " 'Ere's the place for your baggage! Bring it along if you want it weighed; if you don't, it won't go—that's all!"

"Fifteen dollars for you, Sir; forty-six for you, Madam. Seventy-five for you, Miss—heavy trunk, that, Miss."

"Oh dear! oh goodness gracious! must I pay seventy-five dollars for my trunk?" screams the lady.

"Yes, Miss—sorry for it—no getting over it."

"Oh!"

"Quick, Miss—sorry for it—no getting over it."

"Oh!"

"Quick, if you please, ladies and gents! Stage's behind time—won't get to Placerville before dark!"

Then came the final checkup. "Your names, ladies and gents?" The name of every passenger had to be written on the waybill. Or, if the passenger was a foreigner and the driver couldn't catch the spelling, he'd take a quick look at the man to determine his nationality, and then write down "John Chinaman" or "Frenchman" or whatever seemed to fit best, and let it go at that.

Then came the last call. "Pile in, gents. Get down from the front seat—you, Sir—place engaged. All aboard!" Then off the stage would tear.

At the end of a run, no traveler who knew his business ever insulted a driver by giving him a small coin. A nice slouch hat? Yes, that would be "mighty nice"; or a pair of high-cuffed gloves, a fine pair of boots, a silk handkerchief, or good cigars. Such gifts, we are told, were always "acceptable." The drivers usually dressed well and they loved their high boots, patterned gauntlets, and creamy-white hats.

Perhaps, too, such tokens of appreciation for being seemingly snatched from the jaws of death at nearly every turn of the road were given gladly.

No long questionnaire confronted the jehu when seeking a job. As a rule, no references were asked. The proprietor, who knew the right type when he saw it, usually took one good, sharp look at his man and then asked simply and directly:

"Can you drive stage?"

"Yes."

"Can you drive like hell?"

"Yes."

"Do you like to work?"

The proper answer was "Yes."

"Do you drink whisky?"

"No." (At this point he probably lied a little.)

"You're engaged."

Let us now meet some of these interesting knights of the lash. What are their names, their individual characteristics?

There is no telling what names would be given to stage drivers. Some were nicknamed; some were known by their Christian names, others by surnames. It just happened that way. Major Ben. C. Truman had driven with "Mr. Church" many times, and he was always known by that name, plain "Mr. Church." Then there were "Buffalo Jim," the twins, "Curly Dan" and "Curly Jerry" Robbins, "Uncle Jim Miller," "One-Eyed Charlie," "Dutch John," and "Old Shalcross."

At times even newspapers failed to supply the full names of drivers whose exploits were featured. Gordon, Baker, Bowen, Wells, Herd, Ruffin, Pane, Palmer, and Mullen are among those whose last names alone appeared in press. Who many of them really were, their origin, their family connections, will probably never be fully known. On the other hand, there were drivers about whose nomenclature, and even heritage, there remains neither mystery nor doubt.

Billy Carll drove for the California and Oregon Stage Company. He became their northern-division agent during the 'seventies, and he was the sort of person who never went unnoticed. If his personality failed to create a stir, his new suits, hats, gloves, and boots were enough to evoke a spirited squib in the hinterland press. Even a statement from Billy about the weather was of interest. The folks at Yreka were of the impression that whenever Billy drifted in from Oregon it was just "to give his webs a chance to dry."

When sedate President Rutherford B. Hayes and grizzled General William T. Sherman drove through Yreka on the stage, September 26, 1880, it was, of course, Billy Carll who at this point took over the reins from the equally famous and beloved division superintendent, William L. Smith, and drove the presidential party north to Roseburg, Oregon.

As the presidential party arrived it was preceded by another coach which carried inside the reception committee and on top the local brass band, which lustily played *The Star-Spangled Banner*. A long line of coaches and carriages followed. There was loud shouting, but, in keeping with the wishes of the President, there was no "Sunday speechmaking." While welcoming its distinguished guests, Yrekans were at the same time engaged in a frantic search for Siskiyou Mountain robbers who had held up Charley Cramer's stage headed out of Weaverville. Honored as the townspeople were by the presidential visit, they could not refrain from active participation in a man hunt.

During the night the party stayed at Madame Holt's Franco-American Hotel. Madame Holt presented General Sherman with a bill for one hundred dollars on the following morning, with the explanation that "to ze ordinary traveler" the rate was two dollars a day per person, but it was more for "Monsieur Le President, Madame Le President and Monsieur Le General." The hardened veteran of the march through Georgia, flatly refusing to be robbed in so polite a manner, offered Madame Holt fifty dollars, which she accepted.

In his old age Billy Carll secured a contract with the federal government to carry mail in and out of Lakeview for $2,400 a year. Unhappily, one day he was jumped upon by a frightened horse, knocked down, and badly injured. Later he was reported recovering; but, like Crandall and others of this profession, it is ironical that a person who lived with horses all his life should, in the end, become a victim of the creatures he loved so much.

Then there were those jehus who bobbed up everywhere. Such a driver was Billy Hamilton, a man with a fine reputation throughout the entire West. He had driven in California, in Oregon, in Nevada; and thousands of people from far and wide encountered him during his thirty years of driving, which began in 1850.

This short, stout, and jolly driver was once the owner of a line of stages between Colfax and Grass Valley. For a while he owned the Los Angeles to Bakersfield Line, and at still another period of his life he operated his own stage line out of Mojave.

Hamilton liked his drinks, but only when off the job. He made a great deal of money, and was generous to a fault. "I have ridden with Billy in the Sierra, through the Mojave desert, and over the Coast range," recalled Truman, "and considered him one of the most delightful whips in the world." He was well known to Leland Stanford and Charles Crocker. In later life he retired to a farm in Kern County; one of his special delights was to go to San Francisco and stay at the Palace Hotel and play " 'cinch' for half bottles of Extra Dry."

One of the roughest and toughest men ever to drive stage was Clark Foss. A very large and powerful man he was, too, for he was six feet two inches tall and at one time weighed 260 pounds. His hair was heavy and bushy and merged with his equally luxuriant growth of side whiskers. His lip and chin he kept cleanly shaven. And for all his bellicose personality, Foss was a striking and interesting-looking man. At Calistoga his wife operated a hotel, to which Clark always took his hungry passengers for meals. For this the passengers had no regrets, for they ate with relish Mrs. Foss's chicken, game, fruits, vegetables, and tasty desserts. Perhaps best of all were her pure, fresh mountain water and coffee.

It was not Foss's roughness and toughness that bothered passengers but his recklessness. One of his pet stunts was to chain the hind wheels before starting down a steep mountain side and then apply the lash to his team. For this Foss eventually paid a price in damage suits, while others paid with their lives. Foss never drank or smoked, but he swore with such fury that both man and beast feared his oaths.

Much different was his husky, stage-driving son, Charlie, who in temperament was kind and gentle. Before starting his run, Charlie would turn around to look at his passengers and say, "Are you all ready, ladies and gentlemen?"

Stranger than fiction is the life story of Charlie Parkhurst. One of the best-known drivers in California, Charlie drove stage over many runs, among them Stockton to Mariposa, Oakland to San Jose, San Juan to Santa Cruz, and Sacramento to Placerville. On the side this jehu did some farming, worked in the woods, and exhibited endurance and industriousness which everywhere was admired. Always, though, Charlie lived alone.

No passenger of this driver was ever known to have been hurt, although when driving alone one time his coach capsized and "bust in my sides." Browne recalled having ridden in the box with Charlie one dark night from Sacramento to Placerville at a time when the roads were so bad that the horses seemed "to be eternally plunging over precipices and the stage following them with a crashing noise, horribly suggestive of cracked skulls and broken bones." But, says Browne, "I had an implicit confidence in Old Charlie. The way he handled the reins and peered through the clouds and volumes of darkness and saw trees and stumps and boulders of rock and horses' ears, when I could scarcely see my own hand before me was a miracle of stage-driving."

Confident as Browne was, his thoughts turned repeatedly to stories of stages that had crashed in the canyons along which they were then passing. And, turning to Charlie, half frightened, half apologetically, he said:

"Is it possible? . . . ."

"Very likely—they kill 'em quite lively on the Henness route. Git alang, my beauties! . . . . but our company's very strict; they won't keep drivers, as a genr'l thing, that gets drunk and mashes up stages. Git aeoup, Jake! Git alang, Mack! 'Twon't pay; 'taint a good investment for man nor beast."

The stage rolled on.

"How in the world can you see your way through this dust?" asked Browne.

"Smell it. Fact is, I've travelled over these mountains so often I can tell where the road is by the sound of the wheels. When they rattle I'm on hard ground; when they don't rattle I gen'r'lly look over the side to see where she's agoing."

"Have you any other signs?"

"Backer's another sign; when I'm a little skeer'd I chaw more'n ordinary. Then I know the road's bad."

"Don't you get tired driving over the same road so often?"

"Well, I do—kalklate to quit the business next trip. I'm getting well along on in years, you see, and don't like it well as I used to, afore I was busted in!"

"How long have you driven stage?"

"Nigh on to thirty years, an' I'm no better off now than when I commenced. Pay's small; work heavy; gettin' old; rheumatism in the bones; nobody to look out for used-up stage-drivers; kick the bucket one of these days, and that's the last of Old Charlie."

"Why, you must have made plenty of friends during so long a career of staging?"

"Oh yes, plenty of 'em; see 'em to-day, gone to-morrow! Git alang!"

This account was published in 1869. Years passed; Charlie

grew emaciated in appearance; the rheumatism grew worse; and then, from a horse kick in the face, one of his eyes was lost.

For all these handicaps, Charlie, hereafter "One-Eyed Charlie" to newer customers, continued to drive, to like "chewin'," moderate drinking, and a little dice-throwing for cigars.

Then one day Charlie stepped down from the box, turned over the reins to some younger driver, and retired to a little farm near Watsonville, where life was quiet and where the farmers and townspeople alike were kind and friendly. Finally, as if the normal infirmities of old age were not enough, Charlie developed cancer of the tongue, from which death resulted on December 29, 1879.

The body was found by some old friends, and, anxious to give Charlie a decent ride across the Great Divide—which was so much deserved—they prepared the body for burial. It was then, much to the consternation of all, that they discovered that Charlie was a woman. At first there were those who doubted the story; but a statement from a doctor not only confirmed the foregoing fact but attested that the dead woman had been a mother.

Wrote the *Yreka Union*: "There may be a strange history that to a novelist would be a source of inspiration, and again, she may have been disgusted with the trammels surrounding sex, and concluded to work out her fortune in her own way. More light may be thrown on this wonderful case. The female stage driver, Charley Parkhurst, left $4,000 to a little boy who had been kind to her."

Charlie's remains were buried in the Odd Fellows' Cemetery at Watsonville, where her grave can be visited to this day.

While meeting all the requirements of their craft—and talking was not a requisite—some drivers were painfully quiet and self-effacing. Such a man was Sage-Brush Bill. To one traveler who liked to converse, Sage-Brush Bill proved a keen disappointment— so much so that Bill was dubbed William the Silent.

Bill was a lover of horses. He attended strictly to business, and really safe travel required a man of his talents. He fed and watered his horses with tender care; he examined their hoofs and mouths and checked their general health. With a mechanic's instinct he left nothing about the coach unchecked—not a screw, wheel, axle, bolt, strap, or chain. And when the coach rolled into the station one could be sure that Bill, in his silent manner, made every effort to attend to the wishes of his customers.

Bill did not hate Indians, although he had been "burned out" three times by them. He had lost all he had ever owned. On this subject Bill was moved to break his silence and said: ". . . . they didn't leave me a hoof; burnt my cabin; stole my stock; shot me twice—an arrow went through this arm; there's a bullet under this rib—doctor says it has got a case 'round it, and won't hurt me."

Perhaps it was the weight of these tragic experiences that made Bill so quiet and seemingly so sad.

"It is no use fighting any more against such luck as that," he managed to say. And then, as if determined not to admit of defeat: "I shan't pass in my checks till they are called for. I always treated the Indians well, but then others didn't, and that was the trouble."

"Cherokee Bill" was not an Indian but a former white resident of the Western Reserve. Why the name? No one knows. He didn't even look like an Indian. He was short, stout and clumsy, and wore a stub beard. Maybe his slouchy garb, consisting simply of overalls and a dirty woolen shirt, caused his more meticulous colleagues to name this Sierra-driving knight Cherokee Bill. Anyway, he was a strange man, and among the many stories told about him is the following, which comes from the reminiscent pen of Major Truman:

"I was the only passenger except an old clergyman, who occupied the middle seat on the inside. We left Quincy at six in the morning, with not a cloud in the sky. At ten the entire heavens were overcast, it began to sprinkle, and distant muttering of thunder could be heard. At eleven o'clock, when within a thousand feet of the summit, we encountered the full violence of the storm. I had never seen lightning, thunder, and rain, like it. The rain descended not in torrents, but in shafts; the lightning flashed almost incessantly, and the thunders made a continuous roar, with now and then a crash which resembled the fall of a hundred or more of the most noble taxodiums of the forest. I said to Bill, although I was already completely drenched:—

" 'I guess I'll crawl inside.'

" 'No,' he replied, 'you don't want to get in with that thing; he refused to bury my poor boy a few months ago because he hadn't been baptized. I wish one of these pines would strike him dead. He's one of those old duffers who believes that our babies come into the world to be damned and claims that it is wicked to bury a fellow-being if he hasn't been baptized by some old preacher like Kalloch. I'd like to run him off into the cañon.'

"We reached the summit at twelve o'clock, and here a sight presented itself such as I had never seen before. The storm had spent itself on the summit and had been swept into the stupendous chasms surrounding, with all of its celestial pyrotechnics and deafening artillery; and from a sunny elevation seven thousand feet in the air we could behold the jubilee of elements below. I saw Hooker's fight in and about the clouds on Lookout mountain, at the commencement of the Atlanta campaign. I was reminded of that memorable episode by the sight before me, except that, instead of the din of small arms and the infernally-demoralizing 'Rebel yell,' the roar of heaven's artillery in the Sierra that 17th day of August was like that of ten thousand battles in the clouds. Bill reined up so that I could stand and get a good view, at which the passenger stuck his head out of the window and asked:—

" 'What is the matter, driver? What are you stopping here for?'

"Bill was ferocious, and replied, 'I'm listening to the salute the Almighty is firing over my poor boy's grave.'

"The preacher said no more, and I told Bill to drive on, which he did, but quietly said to me: 'Do you think that preacher would ask for my certificate of baptism if he had a chance to bury me? Not much.' "

Cherokee Bill may not have been an Indian, but this does not mean that gentlemen of color were barred from the reins. Definitely not. One of the best-known and best-remembered of all the Sierra drivers was the mulatto, "Alfred"—just plain Alfred. He drove stage in and out of Yosemite and in the course of years probably hauled more important personages than any of his confreres. Grant, Garfield, Hayes, Blaine, Schurz, and Sherman were a few of his many notable customers.

Alfred was well liked and was admired for his immaculate apparel. It is said he wore the "whitest and handsomest" gauntlets of any jehu in the Sierra. When Grant went to Yosemite, he held the reins for a part of the distance and, according to Alfred, smoked four cigars while doing it. The General, however, did not overlook Alfred, to whom he gave a silver-mounted case containing eight cigars. What Grant probably did not know was that he was the only person ever to be permitted by Alfred to take over the reins. Alfred must have known, as so many of his countrymen did, that for all his shortcomings the hero of Appomattox really knew horses.

Like Davy Crockett of Mississippi River fame and lore, the name of Hank Monk has assumed legendary proportions. In real life Hank was by no means a slouch in handling the reins and the whip, and he was well known in staging circles. But that he could drive better and faster than any other jehu in the Sierra is highly questionable, and no such claim was ever made by Monk. Neither was he regarded as highly reliable. Why then was this name on the lips of every Westerner? The cause was the fortuitous meeting of two men, each well known in his own way, each grotesquely different, each adding fame or infamy to the other. These two men were Hank Monk and Horace Greeley, noted editor of the *New York Tribune*.

It was he, Hank Monk, who just chanced to be the man who drove Greeley across the Sierra from Carson City to Placerville at the time the famous editor followed his own advice: "Go West, young man." The year was 1859.

Well, what was so remarkable about that? Many drivers had taken Greeley across the plains and had won no special recognition. Still others had driven personages more famous than Greeley and nothing more than local notoriety came of it.

It all hinges on one apocryphal anecdote and upon conflicting stories as to just how Greeley looked upon reaching Placerville, where a reception committee of rugged pioneers awaited the arrival of their noted New York friend and champion.

In Horace Greeley's own account, *An Overland Journey*, this final lap of the long cross-country stage ride is discussed very casually:

"The road over this pass—here claimed to be the lowest and most practicable over the Sierra Nevada—rises steadily for twelve or thirteen miles from our morning's starting-point, then descends for two or three miles as abruptly to the valley. . . . . But the road, even on this [west] side, is, for most of the way, eaten into the side of a steep mountain, with a precipice of from five to fifteen hundred feet on one side and as steep an eminence on the other. Yet along this mere shelf, with hardly a place to each mile where two meeting wagons can pass, the mail-stage was driven at the rate of ten miles an hour (in one instance eleven), or just as fast as four wild California horses, whom two men could scarcely harness, could draw it."

Exciting? Yes, but nothing unusual in Western stage driving. This was an everyday doing. Even Greeley made nothing special out of Monk. The publisher even failed to mention this driver's name. He simply said:

"Our driver was of course skillful; but had he met a wagon suddenly on rounding one of the sharp points or projections we were constantly passing, a fearful crash was unavoidable. Had his horses seen fit to run away (as they *did* run once, on the un-hooking of a trace, but at a place where he had room to rein them out of the road on the upper side, and thus stop them) I know that he could not have held them, and we might have been pitched headlong down a precipice of a thousand feet, where all of the concern that could have been picked up afterward would not have been two bits per bushel. Yet at this break-neck rate we were driven for not less than four hours or forty miles, changing horses every ten miles, and raising a cloud of dust through which it was difficult at times to see anything. . . . . I cannot conscientiously recommend the route I have traveled to summer tourists in quest of pleasure, but it is a balm for many bruises to know that I am at last in California."

Yes, this was a rugged stretch of road, yet not so dangerous as to claim its victim Hank Monk, who had driven continually back and forth over this run for months. Greeley passed over the road in midsummer, while Monk had driven it in all seasons— in winter when the snow was many feet deep, in blinding blizzards, through driving rain, at times when spring freshets endangered bridges and grades. Yes, Hank Monk had experienced all kinds of weather, and somehow had escaped falling over the cliffs. Moreover, for yet another score of years Hank Monk somehow continued to escape disaster, which to Greeley seemed so imminent on this beautiful, warm, dry August day.

In his *Recollections of a Busy Life,* published nine years later, Greeley chose to omit all reference to Hank Monk. He dwelt instead upon how warm and golden that day was and how a "brawling and leaping" brook followed his Western descent.

Then came the election year of 1872, and "Old Horace," the man who had called all Democrats "traitors," "rebels," and "copperheads," the embattled foe of slavery, became the Democratic standard bearer. His Republican opponent was Ulysses S. Grant.

Resentment toward Greeley came from many quarters, and especially throughout the South. The hostility of the *New York Times* was vicious. But what was most humiliating to Candidate Greeley was the ridicule heaped upon him by three men: two great American humorists, Artemus Ward and Mark Twain, and a cartoonist, Thomas Nast.

Ward visited California soon after Greeley, and this is the story he wrote about the editor's stage ride with Monk at the controls:

"When Mr. Greeley was in California ovations awaited him at every town. He had written powerful leaders in the *Tribune* in favor of the Pacific Railroad, which had greatly endeared him to the citizens of the Golden State. And therefore they made much of him when he went to see them.

"At one town the enthusiastic populace tore his celebrated white coat to pieces, and carried the pieces home to remember him by.

"The citizens of Placerville prepared to fête the great journalist, and an extra coach, with extra relays of horses, was chartered of the California Stage Company to carry him from Folsom to Placerville—distance, forty miles. The extra was in some way delayed, and did not leave Folsom until late in the afternoon. Mr. Greeley was to be fêted at seven o'clock that evening by the citizens of Placerville, and it was altogether necessary that he should be there at that hour. So the Stage Company said to Henry Monk, the driver of the extra, 'Henry, this great man must be there at seven to-night.' And Henry answered, 'The great man shall be there.'

"The roads were in an awful state, and during the first few miles out of Folsom slow progress was made.

" 'Sir,' said Mr. Greeley, 'this is not a trifling matter. I *must* be there at seven!'

"Again came the answer, 'I've got my orders!'

"But the speed was not increased, and Mr. Greeley chafed away another half-hour; when, as he was again about to remonstrate with the driver, the horses suddenly started into a furious run, and all sorts of encouraging yells filled the air from the throat of Henry Monk.

" 'That is right, my good fellow!' cried Mr. Greeley. 'I'll give you ten dollars when we get to Placerville. Now we *are* going!'

"They were indeed, and at a terrible speed.

"Crack, crack! went the whip, and again 'that voice' split the air. 'Git up! Hi Yi! G'long! Yip—Yip!'

"And on they tore over the stones and ruts, up hill and down, at a rate of speed never before achieved by stage horses.

"Mr. Greeley, who had been bouncing from one end of the coach to the other like an India-rubber ball, managed to get his head out of the window, when he said:

" 'Do—on't—on't—on't you—u—u think we—w—e—e shall get there by seven if we do—on't—on't go so fast?'

" 'I've got my orders!' That was all Henry Monk said. And on tore the coach.

"It was becoming serious. Already the journalist was extremely sore from the terrible jolting, and again his head 'might have been seen' at the window.

" 'Sir,' he said, 'I don't care—care—*air*, if we don't get there at seven!'

" 'I have got my orders!' Fresh horses. Forward again, faster than before. Over rocks and stumps, on one of which the coach narrowly escaped turning a summerset.

" 'See here!' shrieked Mr. Greeley. 'I don't care if we don't get there at all!'

" 'I've got my orders! I work for the Californay Stage Company, I do. That's wot I work for. They said, "Git this man through by seving." An' this man's goin' through. You bet! Gerlong! Whoo-ep!'

"Another frightful jolt, and Mr. Greeley's bald head suddenly found its way through the roof of the coach, amidst the crash of small timbers and the ripping of strong canvas.

" 'Stop, you—maniac!' he roared.

"Again answered Henry Monk:

" 'I've got my orders! *Keep your seat, Horace!'*

"At Mud Springs, a village a few miles from Placerville, they met a large delegation of the citizens of Placerville, who had come out to meet the celebrated editor, and escort him into town. There was a military company, a brass band, and a six-horse wagon-load of beautiful damsels in milk-white dresses, representing all the states in the Union. It was nearly dark now, but the delegation were amply provided with torches, and bonfires blazed all along the road to Placerville.

"The citizens met the coach in the outskirts of Mud Springs, and Mr. Monk reined in his foam covered steeds.

" 'Is Mr. Greeley on board?' asked the chairman of the committee.

" He was, a few miles back!' said Mr. Monk. 'Yes,' he added, after looking down through the hole which the fearful jolting had made in the coach-roof—'yes, I can see him! He is there!'

" 'Mr. Greeley,' said the chairman of the committee, presenting himself at the window of the coach, 'Mr. Greeley, sir! We are come to most cordially welcome you, sir—why, God bless me, sir, you are bleeding at the nose!'

" 'I've got my orders!' cried Mr. Monk. 'My orders is as follers: Git him there by seving! It wants a quarter to seving. Stand out of the way!'

" 'But, sir,' exclaimed the committee-man, seizing the off leader by the reins—'Mr. Monk, we are come to escort him into town! Look at the procession, sir, and the brass band, and the people, and the young women, sir!'

" 'I've got my orders!' screamed Mr. Monk. 'My orders don't say nothin' about no brass bands and young women. My orders says, "Git him there by seving!" Let go them lines! Clear the way there! Whoo-ep! Keep your seat, Horace!' and the coach dashed wildly through the procession, upsetting a portion of the brass band, and violently grazing the wagon which contained the beautiful young women in white.

"Years hence, gray-haired men, who were little boys in this procession, will tell their grandchildren how this stage tore through Mud Springs, and how Horace Greeley's bald head ever

"Old Charlie"

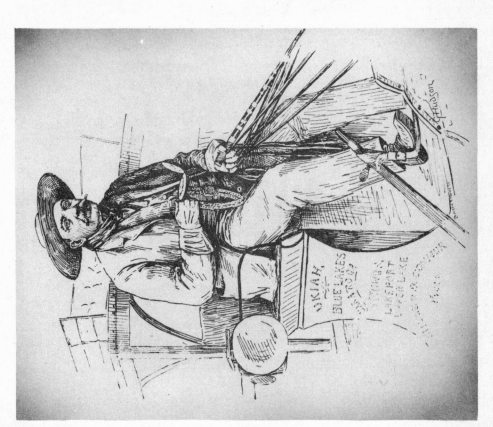

"Uncle Jim Miller"

An early stage driver

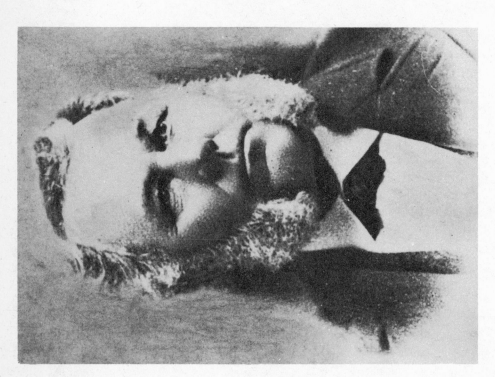

Clark Foss, famous stage driver

and anon showed itself like a wild apparition, above the coach roof.

"Mr. Monk was on time. There is a tradition that Mr. Greeley was very indignant for a while; then he laughed, and finally presented Mr. Monk with a brand new suit of clothes."

Mark Twain went west two years after Greeley and over the same stage route. He stopped at Virginia City, Nevada, where he won fame as a journalist. The humorist relates how out of Julesburg he sat with the driver, who felt an urge to tell a story. And this is the story as related by Mark Twain:

" 'I can tell you a most laughable thing indeed, if you would like to listen to it. Horace Greeley went over this road once. When he was leaving Carson City he told the driver, Hank Monk, that he had an engagement to lecture at Placerville and was very anxious to go through quick. Hank Monk cracked his whip and started off at an awful pace. The coach bounced up and down in such a terrific way that it jolted the buttons all off of Horace's coat, and finally shot his head clean through the roof of the stage, and then he yelled at Hank Monk and begged him to go easier—said he warn't in as much of a hurry as he was awhile ago. But Hank Monk said, "Keep your seat, Horace, and I'll get you there on time"—and you bet you he did, too, what was left of him!' "

Then a couple of days passed and a man from Denver was taken aboard the stage. He talked of this and that for a while and then said:

" 'I can tell you a most laughable thing indeed, if you would like to listen to it. Horace Greeley went over this road once. When he was leaving Carson City he told the driver, Hank Monk, ...' "

At Fort Bridger Mark Twain heard the identical story from another man; out from Salt Lake he heard it from still another. It was near Ragtown, however, that the pay-off occurred. There by the roadside the passengers found a man in the agonies of death. He was taken aboard, momentarily revived with brandy, and then, "in a feeble voice that had a tremble of honest emotion in it: 'Gentleman, I know not who you are, but you saved my life; and although I can never be able to repay you for it, I feel that I can at least make one hour of your long journey lighter. . . . . I can tell you a most laughable thing indeed, if you would like to listen to it. Horace Greeley——' "

"Suffering stranger," said Mark Twain, "proceed at your peril."

In a footnote at the end of this chapter Mark Twain adds: "And what makes that worn anecdote the more aggravating is, that the adventure it celebrates *never occurred.*"

Stories as to Greeley's condition upon arriving in Placerville began circulating and they grew in the retelling. Even as late as 1886 when Major Truman visited Placerville he inquired of his innkeeper about Greeley. Oh! Greeley! The innkeeper remembered well, for it was at his place that the publisher had stayed. The account was polished and refined from many years of repeating.

The canvas top of the coach had been torn in two or three places and Greeley's hat was knocked in. The team was white with foam, while the coach, driver, and passenger were covered with dust and mud.

All told, Horace Greeley was much abused and in the process of making him look ridiculous Hank Monk was given nationwide notoriety. Before the stories began circulating, Greeley certainly bore no animosity toward Monk, to whom the editor presented a gold watch. In later years Monk pawned this watch many times —probably for twenty-rod whisky—but somehow always managed to redeem it. Monk had also liked Greeley. In contradiction to this story, one will remember that Artemus Ward reported that it was a new suit of clothes which Monk received. Maybe it was both. It was not until in later years when the anecdote had been widely circulated that Greeley, in reply to a request of Monk for some favor, said: "I would rather see you 10,000 fathoms in Hell than ever give you a crust of bread, for you are the only man who ever had the opportunity to place me in a ridiculous light, and you villainously exercised that opportunity, you damned scamp."

Hank lived on until 1883 as the most famous of all jehus. When death came the press notices were numerous. "In his way, Hank Monk was a character," wrote the Virginia City *Enterprise.* "In the old days, before the leathers under his coach were soaked with alcohol, there was no better balanced head than his. . . . . In his prime he would turn a six horse coach in the street with the team at a full run, and with every line apparently loose.

But the coach would always bring up in exactly the spot that the most careful driver would have tried to bring it. . . . . His driving was such a perfection of art that it did not seem art at all, and many an envious whip, watching him, has turned away to say 'He is the luckiest man that ever climbed on top of a box.' "

The *Redding Independent* made a very brief comment about Monk's passing. "Old Shasta pioneers will remember Mr. Monk, as we understand that he once lived within the borders of the county that has been made famous by having been the home of many who have won fame in various callings."

To all the West—yes, to all Americans who love the memory of the rampaging West—the story of Hank Monk and Horace Greeley—factual or fictional—will always be cherished.

By and large the traveling public loved and respected the stagecoach drivers. There were no notices posted on coaches saying: "Do not talk to the operator." As a class, the jehus were sociable and accommodating. Many letters such as the following from a lady passenger were received by the management:

"The drivers are thorough gentlemen, and look to the comfort and pleasure of their passengers to the utmost of their ability. When ladies are traveling alone, this is a very important fact, and tends greatly to the removal of unpleasant features of such necessity. Having traveled from Redding to Jacksonville, Oregon, and ridden with ten different drivers on the road I had quite an opportunity to judge of their qualifications, and it affords me great pleasure, ... to testify to their uniform courtesy, their genial dispositions and their thoughtful care for the comfort of passengers. Some of them possess a fund of wit and humor which render a ride with them a most entertaining one."

Somehow, would-be travelers found the staging and stage driving unique in California. Nowhere else did they encounter the "breakneck speed"; nowhere else did they find so many precipitous mountain passes where stage traffic was so heavy. In tribute to the drivers, John W. Boddam-Whetham, famed English traveler, wrote of the "knowingness and sure-footedness" as well as the "brilliant attainments of the 'knights of the whip.'" They may as a class have been consummate liars; but, as drivers of galloping teams, they knew their trade.

Chapter 6

THROW DOWN THAT BOX!

OLD-RUSH CALIFORNIA WAS A magnet for all manner of scoundrels. They poured into San Francisco from Australia, from the Far East, from the American frontier, and, in fact, from all corners of the earth. Soon they fanned out into other mushroom towns, and urban California became the scene of operations for hoodlums, "hounds," "Sydney ducks," "con" men, and organized gangs of ruffians and cutthroats.

For about two years the expressmen and the traveling public escaped much of this curse of outlawry. Then late in 1851 it struck—suddenly, without warning. A band of robbers, headed by "Charley Smith," began operations in Shasta Valley, and from the southern mines also came reports of roadside holdups.

Men engaged in highway robbery were commonly known as road agents. They were in a class by themselves, for special techniques and the utmost bravado were required of them. It took no special skill for a Sydney hoodlum to shoot a man in the back as he walked unsuspectingly down a darkened San Francisco street. On the other hand, to stride boldly forth from a roadside thicket to halt and rob an oncoming stagecoach took, at least for a lone hand, iron nerves and skill. Some road agents operated in large groups when perpetrating their holdups. Sometimes they slaughtered outright innocent victims. But if the agent had iron nerve, a strong commanding voice, and a shotgun to point in the direction of the driver's seat, shooting was considered unnecessary roughness.

Perhaps the easiest target of highwaymen was the lone expressman who made his way down solitary mountain trails. Slowly moving packers were also vulnerable to attack. Even so, the cases of robbery on record up to 1855 are relatively few considering the hundreds of pack trains, expressmen, and stages which by then almost choked California's dirt roads.

A Dillon and Company's stage was robbed in 1851; but not until April 1852 did a really first-class highway robbery occur. Near Illinoistown, men of Reelfoot Williams' short-lived gang swooped down upon a stage and deprived the driver of his express box containing $7,500.

A prominent member of this gang was Dick Barter, better known as Rattlesnake Dick. He was so called because of his associations with Rattlesnake Bar, where he had tried his luck at mining and had failed. Suspected of thefts of which the court found him innocent, the sensitive and vengeful Dick Barter decided to pursue a life of crime. In addition to becoming a road agent, he began robbing whenever an opportunity presented itself. In 1855, as a member of a gang, Rattlesnake Dick helped attack a heavily guarded Trinity County mule train carrying $80,000 of Wells, Fargo and Company gold.

Throughout the 'fifties Dick committed one crime after another, until one night in July 1859 the law caught up with him. He was shot while attempting to escape arrest near Auburn, and the next morning his dead body was found some distance away at a roadside with two bullet holes in his chest and one through his head. There is still disagreement about the head wound. Is it possible that Rattlesnake Dick, realizing that the end of his career of crime had come, administered his own *coup de grace?* Or did a companion perform this last rite? Certain it is that if a bullet from his pursuer's gun had entered his head, the victim would have fallen dead in his tracks.

Stagecoach robberies failed to become a great public menace until about 1856, when the once-handsome, swaggering, egotistical, and highly literate "Dr." Thomas J. Hodges, alias Tom Bell, made his debut on California's roads. Tom came from Rome, Tennessee. He received a training in medicine, served honorably in the Mexican War, and then joined the great rush to California. Luck failed him at the diggings, and Tom sought consolation in drink and cards. His excessive drinking frequently resulted in brawls, one of which left Tom with a badly crushed nose. For the future road agent this made identification embarrassingly easy. Eventually, though, Tom turned to robbery, was caught, and went to prison in 1855. He was not long in effecting his escape and, moreover, in resuming the trade of bandit. As hangouts he chose Mountaineer House on the Folsom-Auburn road, also frequented by Rattlesnake Dick, the popular California House on the Camptonville road out from Marysville, and Hog Ranch near the Nevada City road. Hog Ranch was operated by redheaded Elizabeth Hood, who had three daughters, the eldest of whom, only fourteen years of age, Tom Bell is reported to have loved.

The pattern of operations followed by Tom Bell became well known. At first he generally traveled alone, and, for boldness, wrote the *San Francisco Bulletin,* he was "second only to Joaquin Murietta," whose sinister exploits were not so much connected with staging as with the mining towns. It was believed that for protection Tom wore a coat of armor under his clothes. He did not shoot unless it was necessary. By 1856 Tom Bell sought to expand his operations by organizing a gang, and one active lieutenant was Bill Gristy, alias Bill White, an escaped convict.

There was some humanity about Tom Bell, although this could scarcely be said of Gristy and others in the gang. One time a lone traveler on the Downieville-Marysville road was held up by Bell and Gristy. The traveler tried to flee, but Gristy shot his victim in the leg and stopped him. After removing whatever money there was, "Dr." Bell is said to have dressed the injured leg and ordered Gristy to stop an approaching wagon, into which the patient was carefully placed. Bell then instructed the driver of the wagon to "drive slow and pick your road."

Tom and his gang operated throughout the northern mines. Their list of crimes was lengthy; but the most famous holdup was the robbery of Sam Langton's stage on August 12, 1856. From one of his scouts Tom learned that a particular Langton stage had aboard a treasure box containing $100,000 in gold and that the stage was transporting only about eight passengers, five of whom were not likely to resist in the event of a holdup. Seated with driver John Gear, however, was Bill Dobson, a "shotgun messenger" sent along by Sam Langton to guard the treasure. In view of this, Tom took along seven of his toughest men for the job. With Dobson aboard it would not be easy, he "calculated," and circumstances proved his doubts warranted.

When Tom Bell and his cohorts swooped out on the road, Gear had no choice but to slow up. Dobson was under no such compunction, and like a flash this courageous man began firing upon at least five of the gang. Having unloaded his shotgun, Dobson flashed his pistol and resumed fire. By his courage Dobson saved the day. Tom Bell was unhorsed, and the rest, overcome by the unexpected turn of events, fled. No less than forty shots had been exchanged; Gear was shot in the arm, one passenger was hit in the legs, and a Negro woman had been shot in the head and killed. Four Chinese passengers and one white had jumped from the stage and had fled unharmed. Brave Dobson escaped without a scratch, his prompt action having saved the $100,000 treasure. It is not surprising that the grateful Langton presented his messenger with a gold watch and in other ways expressed appreciation.

California vigilantes and the law were making it tough for outlaws by the middle 'fifties. Following the Langton express affair, the noose began tightening on the Bell gang. The *Calaveras Chronicle* reported in September 1856 that "Our country now contains five of Tom Bell's freebooters." The hangouts had become known to the law and a raid on Mountaineer House had netted the biggest catch. "From the exertions that are being made by the authorities, and the success that attends their efforts, we have reason to hope that this formidable gang will soon be broken up," concluded the *Chronicle*.

This hope was amply realized. In a restaurant at Knight's Ferry, Gristy and a Mexican partner were recognized, arrested, and thrown into a store jail. The next day Gristy revealed to his captors the hideout of Tom Bell. It was given as none other than Elizabeth Hood's Hog Ranch. When the posse arrived at the ranch, members of the gang were there, but not Tom. Before another week passed, however, he was sighted by mere chance. A man on horseback had been seen in a thicket off a roadside, obviously trying to avoid being seen. Upon this clue the posse acted; it rode to the spot and, to the surprise of all, there was Tom Bell, still sitting in the saddle.

Tom had not moved when he heard the galloping horses approaching, for little did he realize that his whereabouts was known. Thus taken by surprise, resistance seemed futile. Tom Bell, the road agent, had reached the end of his trail. He was given four hours in which to arrange the final affairs of his unhappy life.

During this time Tom wrote a letter to Mrs. Hood in which he said that he had been "most foully betrayed" and that every robbery that had been committed during the preceding twelve months had been attributed to him. For these he must "die like a dog." He then wrote: "I must come to a close, for the hounds are thirsting for my Blood. Good Bye, forever. Thos. J. Bell."

He also wrote a brief letter to his mother in which he sent greetings to old friends back in Tennessee and admonished them "never to enter into any gambling saloon, for that has been my ruin. . . . . Your only boy, Tom."

Under the gallows—a rope thrown unceremoniously over the limb of a sycamore by his captors—Tom "prayed fervently." As he did so the noose was placed around his neck, and, without due process of law, he was pulled skyward. A few minutes later the Stockton sheriff arrived, probably content that the state had been spared the cost of a trial. Few tears were shed for Tom Bell; but there were those who objected mildly—always mildly—to another execution without judicial procedure.

Liquidation of the Bell gang slowed up highway robbery for a while, but by no means did it vanish. Reports of road-agent activities continued to come from all parts of California for many years to come. Even in Tom Bell's bailiwick one reads in the *Marysville Enquirer* how a "California Stage Company's coach, going from this city to Rabbit Creek, was stopped by three desperate villains, for the purpose of plunder." The bandit leader leveled his shotgun at Ned Winchel, the driver, and pulled the trigger. Fortunately, a heavy rain had soaked the powder, which failed to explode. Winchel, meanwhile, brought his gun into action and there came an exchange of shots between him and the other bandits. The assailants were dispersed, and the stage, except for holes in the driver's seat, came safely through to Marysville.

A most daring robbery of the Auburn-Folsom stage occurred during the early hours on May 3, 1858. Six armed men stopped the coach and took possession of the Wells, Fargo and Company box containing $21,585.25. Not long after, at Yankee Jim's, an express box containing $7,314.25 was stolen at the stage depot just as the treasure was to have been placed aboard the stage. During September 1858, near Forest City, a stagecoach was held up, but the road agents this time found an empty treasure box and failed to get the sack under the back seat, which contained $15,000.

The year 1859 opened with a robbery of the Forest Hill stage by no less than seven or eight disguised men—"who sprang out from a clump of trees, some seizing the horses, and two upon either side of the stage, with revolvers cocked and almost touching the persons of the messenger and driver, demanded the treasure box." The next day the broken box, some untouched letters, and masks were found at the scene by detectives of Wells, Fargo and Company.

As a rule, the road agents made their escape from the scene of action; but such was not the case at Yankee Jim's when on November 8, 1859, four men stopped the stage and demanded "the treasure" of the driver. At this point two passengers from inside the coach opened fire and each killed his man. Then, stepping out of the stage, they resumed fire and wounded a third and possibly a fourth.

Robberies also continued throughout the decade of the 'sixties, and the pattern for them remained the same. The main interest of road agents appears to have been the treasure box, not the mail bags and not the valuables passengers might carry. Road agents worked fast, and why should they run added risks by searching passengers when the "big stuff" was in the box? Often it was their practice to cache their loot until excitement had died down. One story is told regarding the robbery of Sam D. Brastow's stage by six men in 1856. The amount taken was $25,000, and the loot was hidden. Five of the six men were caught and given ten-year sentences. Upon their release three of these men went at once to the scene of their crime. It was believed that they recovered the cached plunder and vanished.

Not all road agents were accorded the privilege of returning to their hidden treasure, but instead were hanged. Rumors persist to this very day that thousands of dollars worth of gold still lie hidden beneath some lonely granite rock in the Siskiyous and the Sierra. But just where? That is the mystery that adds spice to the retelling.

California has a rightful claim to the most-publicized road agent the West has ever known. Beginning in 1875, and for a period of eight years thereafter, a mysterious figure known to the public as "Black Bart, the Po 8," successfully robbed twenty-seven stagecoaches. Following his twenty-eighth attempt he was caught, tried, convicted, and sentenced to a six-year term of imprisonment in California's San Quentin penitentiary.

"Black Bart" was known and recognized solely by his dress and his masterful technique. His most effective asset was his deep, resonant, commanding voice, which never failed to leave the man at the reins incapable of performing any other act than obligingly tossing out the Wells Fargo treasure box from under the driver's seat.

His unique outward garb consisted of a light-colored duster and a white flour sack over his head, with openings for his striking blue eyes. Bart felt his way very carefully before attempting a holdup. He first would learn the lay of the land. By casually visiting around in some mining town, perhaps posing as a miner or promoter, he would learn of gold shipments slated to be sent by stage. He would observe, if possible, where the box would be placed, who the passengers would be, and then hasten to the scene selected for action. Suitable spots, preferably near the crest of a hill, where the going was slow for the team, were chosen as most desirable places for the holdups. Out of the wayside bushes, shotgun in hand, he would stride confidently in front of the coach. The startled horses would come to an abrupt halt, providing Black Bart with a shield around which he would point his gun directly into the face of the alarmed and dumfounded driver. Once the express box was thrown out on the roadside, and in Bart's case, the mail bags, too, the driver was permitted to take his hasty departure. He never once robbed the passengers, though folklore has it when an excited woman tossed him her purse he courteously returned it to her intact.

At or near the scene of the crime he never failed to leave ransacked boxes and bags, the latter always characteristically slit open in a "T." As if anxious to leave additional identification, this intrepid robber left snatches of poetry in each of the first two

Wells, Fargo and Company boxes that he so ceremoniously emptied. Reads one:

> here I lay me down to Sleep
> to wait the coming morrow
> perhaps Success perhaps defeat
> And everlasting Sorrow
>
> I've labored long and hard for bred
> for honor and for riches
> But on my corns too long yove tred
> You fine haired — — —
>
> let come what will I'll try it on
> My condition cant be worse
> and if theres money in that Box
> Tis munny in my purse
>
> Black Bart
the. Po 8

Not only California, but all the West was agog. The money stolen belonged principally to miners from all parts of the coast, and the mails contained undisclosed amounts in checks and currency from all parts of the world—not to mention the long-awaited letters from home. Black Bart had a propensity for distributing his lone-handed operations over vast areas, and the official record lists four of his holdups as having been of stagecoaches bound from Roseburg, Oregon, to either Yreka or Redding, California.

Black Bart's twenty-eighth, and last, highway drama occurred out from Sonora, California, near the crest of Funk Hill, four or five miles from the mining town of Copperopolis. It was November 3, 1883. Reason E. McConnell was the driver of the Nevada Stage Company coach. To forestall just such acts as those perpetrated by the mysterious Po 8, the Wells Fargo box was not placed under the driver's seat this time but instead was fastened to the bottom of the coach in the passenger compartment. In it were $550 in gold, some gold dust, and 228 ounces of amalgam. The only passenger that morning was "Mister McConnell's" friend, young Jimmy Rolleri, who was "hitching a ride" on the empty stage, and planning to go "ahuntin'," or at any rate had taken his Henry rifle with him in case there was "sumpin'" to shoot at. Since nothing appeared within view of his perch on the box with the driver, Jimmy decided to get off and try to scare up some game around the side of Funk Hill and then rejoin McConnell on the far side. This, then, was the setting for the final holdup of the West's most famous desperado.

Near the crest of the hill Black Bart, true to form, strode out from hiding, shotgun in hand, robed in his duster, the flour sack over his head, and wearing a Derby hat. This time, however, the situation did not fit the customary pattern, and there were some elements perturbing to the leading actor. First, the boy. Where was he? Bart had seen him on the stage. Second, the box. Securely locked and fastened to the floor inside the coach, the treasure box demanded special handling. McConnell was forced to get down, unhitch his horses, and drive them over the crest of the hill and remain there. So far so good, but never in his previous twenty-seven robberies had there been so much time spent during which plans could go awry.

Black Bart worked fast and desperately at opening the box, but over the summit McConnell was not idle. He managed to attract Jimmy's attention and warned him of trouble, for the boy had the only weapon for a counterattack. After finally extracting the loot, the robber backed out of the coach door, but just as he did so McConnell and Jimmy, who had by then joined forces, sneaked up over the hump of the hill and saw the perfect target which Bart presented. Jimmy's new Henry rifle blazed away, not once but three times. It is not known whether Jimmy alone, or both men, shot the gun. The third time a hit was scored just as the hooded phantom faltered and vanished into the brush.

When James B. Hume, detective for Wells, Fargo and Company, heard of this affair he had reason to be elated. Perhaps Black Bart had been seriously wounded and would seek medical attention. Perhaps in his departure under fire Bart might have left new scraps of evidence which would further develop the picture already well outlined in Hume's mind. This time the detective was handsomely rewarded, for among the evidence collected were Bart's Derby hat, a magnifying glass, a case for field glasses, and a handkerchief. And what a clue the handkerchief furnished! In one corner appeared the laundry mark "F.X.O.$_7$." During a hasty checkup with ninety-one San Francisco laundries it was learned that this was the mark assigned to a C. E. Bolton, who lived in Room 40, 37 Second Street, San Francisco.

The owner of the handkerchief was located, and from various other bits of descriptive evidence was identified as the pleasant stranger seen in the neighborhood of the most recent stage robbery. Arrested, Bolton, alias Boles, alias Black Bart, attempted to bluff his way out. Hoping for leniency, when tried before the judge he confessed to having robbed McConnell's stage and received a six-year sentence as prisoner number 11,046 at San Quentin.

About the mystery-shrouded figure who had so aroused the entire West, Hume had the following to say in his official report:

"Bolton, Charles E., *alias* C. E. Boles, *alias* 'Black Bart,' the P.O. 8.

"Nativity, New York; County, Calaveras; Age, 55 years; Occupation, Miner; Height, 5 feet 7½ inches; Complexion, Light; Color of eyes, Blue; Color of hair, Gray; . . . . heavy eyebrows, chin square, rather small, two upper front teeth on right side gone, two lower center teeth gone, small mole on left cheek bone . . . . gunshot wound on right side of navel."

This was not at all the anticipated description of a youthful, dashing, romantic figure, and the gentlemen of the press saw their beautiful legend collapse. The disappointment of both press and public, however, was mitigated somewhat by Hume's statements on Bolton's interesting personality:

"He is a person of great endurance, a thorough mountaineer, and a remarkable walker, and claims that he cannot be excelled in making quick transits over mountains and grades; when reading without glasses, holds paper off at arms length; is comparatively well educated, a general reader, and is well informed on current topics; cool, self-contained, a sententious talker, with waggish tendencies; and since his arrest has, upon several occasions, exhibited genuine wit, under most trying circumstances. Has made his head-quarters in San Francisco for past eight years; has made but few close friends, and those of first-class respectability; is neat and tidy in dress, highly respectable in appearance, and extremely proper and polite in behaviour, chaste in language, eschews profanity, and has never been known to gamble, other than buying pools on horse races and speculating in mining stocks."

There were holdups later which some accredited to Black Bart, but there is no conclusive evidence that he was involved. Actually the bandit vanished from public notice after his release from prison; but from that day to this a new legend has formed about the Po 8 who at one time had been the terror of the road. An old stagecoach, supposed to have been held up for the Wells Fargo treasure box it carried, is carefully preserved today at Knott's Berry Farm, a popular eating place near Los Angeles. On a wooden plaque describing the historic experiences of the old Concord is this solemn inscription:

"HIS GHOST RETURNS

"It is reported that Black Bart had a curious and intense liking for this perticular coach & though he has been dead these 40 odd years, there are some who say that his spirit often returns here.

"And on nights when there is no moon, he can be actually seen lounging quite comfortable in the interior of this coach, & on occasion he sometimes climbs up into the drivers seat & plies the whip to the horses so vehemently that the coach & all go clattering down the road at a tremendous speed as though a hundred thousand (100,000) highwayman were going to kill him and steal all the Gold he had so boldly taken during his adventurous lifetime."

Black Bart so dominated the crime publicity of the late 'seventies and early 'eighties that historians have all but ignored Bart's contemporaries. Bart set a high standard for efficiency and production, but he by no means achieved a monopoly. During September 1875, the year Bart began his career, an Oregon-bound stage found its path blocked in the Siskiyou Mountains. Driver Milo Mathews, accompanied by a Wells Fargo agent, stopped. Then from out of the roadside brush came the familiar command: "Throw out the express box!" Milo was not one to be perturbed by such mild-mannered tactics and simply growled his reply: "Go to hell." Meanwhile, the two men cleared away the road block, got back on their seats, and drove off at "a lively gait." A week later the road agent was identified; but, according to the report, "the rascal, finding he was wanted, made tracks for some safer region of the country, probably Oregon."

It would almost appear that Black Bart's successful exploits served as an inducement to prospective road agents, some timid and others perfectly willing to show their colors. "Scarcely a week passes by," wrote the *Trinity Journal,* "but the story comes to us from some quarter—now on one route then on another—that the stage has been robbed. . . . . The success attending these attacks is such as to encourage others to the nefarious business, the treasure-box of Wells, Fargo & Co. generally giving the robbers a pretty fair dividend, while the difficulty of capturing and convicting the robbers makes the business an apparently safe one."

This newspaper pleaded for immediate legislative enactment leading to surer and sterner punishment, meaning death. This increased vigilance and zeal did not always prove to be the correct answer, for cases on record for the 'seventies show that men were sometimes nearly lynched or barely escaped capital punishment for highway robberies they did not commit.

Statements concerning other robberies committed in the Pacific Northwest, robberies which involved loss of Wells, Fargo and Company treasure, are found in other reports of Detective Hume. Among these cases are reports on Tom Brown, alias "Tom Foster," George Bouldin, and Benjamin Berry. Another respectable citizen turned road agent was William Briscoe, a deputy sheriff, who robbed the Wells, Fargo and Company's express on a stage going from Grants Pass, Oregon, to Jacksonville on January 18, 1884. For this Briscoe served an eight-year term in Oregon's state penitentiary. Briscoe had two accomplices, one of whom, Charles Bassett, received a similar sentence.

And so the robberies continued. Early in June 1876 the California and Oregon Stage was robbed, but in this case the agent was apprehended a few days later. The same stage company was robbed by three men in August, with a loss of more than $4,000. Again in November three men attacked what turned out to be Ben Holladay's private coach, in which Holladay and his wife and William L. Smith, division agent for the Oregon and California Line, were passengers. The box was taken and the mail sack was emptied and thrown back into the stage, but the passengers were unmolested. This took place on a Friday. On the following Monday the agents struck again, and still again on Thursday. Each time the treasure box was demanded and each holdup meant the loss of a considerable sum of money.

Tough as they were, teamsters also fell prey to banditry. Not all of the stories recorded, however, were *bona fide,* for men of this class found the holdup gag the easiest explanation for losses at the gaming table. The real "sufferers," we are told, "were almost invariably those who were careless in handling or talking about their wealth." Road agents were usually smart, well-informed men, and they knew well in advance who had money and where it was kept.

Unlike the jehus, teamsters could not apply the lash and "drive furiously" to escape in the event of a holdup. Their method of dealing with the bandits is best illustrated by the following story:

In a certain tavern barroom, gathered over their drinks, were several mule skinners and bullwhackers.

"What would you do, Sandy Dan"—Daniel Daly was his real name—"if you ever got stuck up?"

"No one man will ever rob me unless he kills me," was Sandy Dan's quick reply.

"That's all right," said another; "but I'll tell you, when one man points a gun at your head and demands your money, he looks mighty big, and the longer you look at him the more he grows, until you begin to think he is a whole army with artillery thrown in. I think, Dan, you would weaken, same as I did, and do the same as nearly everybody does."

"I might, but I don't think so."

The next morning the teamsters were out on the road. Sandy Dan alone headed toward the mines; the others went in the opposite direction. He had no sooner passed from view of his comrades than a masked man stepped out from some bushes, his pistol pointed at the teamster's head.

Sandy Dan, who was riding a lead horse, brought his animals to an abrupt halt and looked through the holes of the mask into the eyes of the robber. At the same time he let the butt of his blacksnake whip slip through his hand and took a firm grip on the lash's end.

Impatiently the robber ordered, "Throw out your money or I'll blow out your brains."

Tiburcio Vasquez and the cabin which was the scene of his capture

James B. Hume, famous Wells Fargo detective

Courtesy Wells Fargo Historical Museum

A Wells, Fargo and Company reward circular

Black Bart, California's most notorious road agent

"You wouldn't attempt this if you were alone," replied Dan. "I am alone and I'll pull the trigger if you don't hurry up."

"Who is that fellow coming there?" asked Sandy Dan, looking beyond the robber's head.

At this point the gunman made his fatal error. As he turned to look, the butt of Dan's whip, heavily laden with lead, came crashing down upon the road agent's head. He dropped to his knees, and the pistol fell from his hand. Then Sandy Dan leaped from his saddle, fell upon the dazed man, and mauled him into unconsciousness. Tying the wretch hand and foot, Dan threw him on his wagon and hauled him back to the authorities at Marysville.

It was some time before the bandit recovered. He was tried, sentenced to ten years at San Quentin, "where," as if the story needed a moral, "he had plenty of time to reflect on the folly of doubting a teamster's nerve."

Perhaps the meanest scoundrel and brute ever to wield a gun in California was the mestizo Tiburcio Vasquez. The victims of this cruel man were from many parts in central and southern California. Murieta was a cutthroat, but he was at least refined in the art of killing. Vasquez was neither refined nor discriminating, although one might not have expected more from a person who began murdering and "betraying damsels" at the tender age of fifteen.

Although given more to horsethieving than to highway robbery, Vasquez was by no means a stranger, and he was always a dread to California drivers and teamsters of the late 'sixties and early 'seventies. In league with "Red-handed Dick" Procopio and Juan Soto, he terrorized the Bay area during the summer of 1870. And in doing so he did not leave the stages unscathed. Following this outburst, he and some other cohorts attacked the Visalia stage near Soap Lake, in which performance they robbed the occupants and tossed them, tightly bound, into a field near by. The agents then drove the stage around a hill, moved on toward Hollister, and robbed three or four teamsters. As if this were not enough for a day's work, Vasquez personally deprived Thomas McMahon, Hollister's leading merchant, of $750 in gold.

This time Vasquez left a hot trail behind him. Overtaken by the constable of Santa Cruz, Vasquez fought a gun battle during which both contestants were severely wounded. Although bleeding badly, Vasquez made his getaway and rode sixty miles to his hideout in Cantua Canyon.

Such were the deeds of Vasquez, and they continued on an even grander scale until May 14, 1874, when he was trapped by a posse in a rude house near Los Angeles. Even then, hopelessly surrounded and outnumbered, the desperado made a wild rush for his horse. Before he reached it, a bullet struck him. He returned fire; then, realizing that the game was up, he raised his hands, walked bleeding to his captors, and with a smile said: "Boys, you have done well; I have been a damned fool." At San Jose on March 19, 1875, he paid with his life on the gallows.

All told, the number of holdups—some successful, some not— was appalling throughout the 'seventies and 'eighties. In an effort to combat this menace, the express companies employed an ever-increasing number of quick-on-the-draw shotgun messengers. There is no way of measuring the contribution of these courageous men who risked their lives for the service. How many robberies they forestalled will never be known, but that their presence on the driver's box deterred many an attempt there can be little doubt.

Some messengers never came to grips with their hidden enemies. One such person was James Otey Bradford, who tells us in his memoirs that he always kept his guns handy but says nothing about being attacked. Another was John Brent. In a brief biographical sketch prepared by Wells, Fargo and Company for use at the Columbian Exposition in Chicago in 1892, one reads: "Brent was exceedingly fortunate the time of his service with the Company, never having been requested to hold up his hands. . . . ." Brent credited his own good fortune to "not having any confidants and invariably keeping his own and the Company's business to himself." Moreover, it was his policy as a chief messenger to make the treasure shipments in coaches which carried no passengers. Thus the decks were cleared for action, and road agents knew it. There was nothing that a bandit wished more than to have women and children aboard a coach marked for robbery. In such cases the messengers most generally obliged the road agent by dropping their guns and by lifting their hands skyward while the drivers brought their horses to a halt. It was Brent's feeling that when he faced "his Maker" he did not wish to account for the deaths of innocent people.

Certainly Wells Fargo had one messenger who was given an opportunity to display his daring and skill, and that was George Hackett. The stage carrying express between Forbestown and Marysville was robbed by two masked men on June 20, 1879. They secured $620 in gold dust and some coin. The next day a stage going from Forest City to Marysville met the two masked men. But this time Hackett sat on the box in readiness. Without the slightest hesitation he raised his shotgun, and, before he could fire, the men disappeared. Hackett jumped from the box and ran in search of the men. When he had gone about 200 yards, he came upon the camp where they had left many of their clothes—in fact, it looked to Hackett as if they must have attempted to commit robbery in their underclothes.

Though vulnerable to attack, Hackett proceeded to examine the camp. He found there a valise containing the $620 stolen the previous day. In the bandits' trousers was $256 in coin. Without further ado, the messenger gathered up the loot and dashed for the stage, which meanwhile had been halted. Tossing the recovered treasure aboard, he ordered the driver to proceed to a safer position. Hackett himself went back to the brush and found one of the robbers who had returned for his clothes. Hackett then covered the man and promptly secured his arrest; his conviction followed and a fifteen-year sentence in the penitentiary. The second of the pair escaped.

Considering how vulnerable Hackett had been to attack, this deed is recalled as one of the most daring on record.

That Hackett was quick on the draw one highwayman learned near Laporte on July 13, 1882. Again Hackett was on the box with the driver, and again a man stepped forward with intent to rob. "Quick as a flash," reads the official account of this episode, "Hackett fired at him, the ball grazing his head. The robber then pointed his gun at the driver, but before he could pull the trigger, a second shot well directed from Hackett knocked the gun out of the would-be robber's hands, upon which he took to his heels, falling down at the start and dropping his hat and mask which were picked up by the victor as battle trophies." Who this road agent actually was did not become known until much later, when the notorious Black Bart confessed that it was he who on that July day on the Laporte road had escaped so narrowly.

Counter measures did not always prove so successful. Occasionally a shotgun messenger scored a hit; generally he did not. But, as Dick Fellows, one of the smoothest of the road agents, wrote before entering Folsom: "Crime. It don't pay." As a rule a road agent ultimately reached the end of his trail either behind the bars or at the end of a rope.

In collaboration with detective John N. Thacker, Hume published a report on robberies involving the Wells, Fargo and Company for the period of 1875 to 1883. It lists no less than 206 convictions for robbery through the area in which the company operated. Only eleven road agents were killed resisting arrest, and only seven were officially hanged. For all their encounters with holdup men, the jehus and passengers fared better than the law of averages would seem to allow. Only four of each died of shots from a road agent's gun, although many more were wounded.

This, it must be emphasized, was a report concerning Wells, Fargo and Company only. There were many other express and stagecoach companies involved in holdups, but no such record as Hume's and Thacker's is available to help complete the picture.

Chapter 7

THE END OF THE TURBULENT 'FIFTIES

WHEN THE SOUTH SECEDED AND THE nation became torn with civil strife, California chose to remain loyal to the Union. By then she had an impressive population of 379,994, widely distributed throughout the state.

Farming, manufacturing, and commerce now thrived as never before; but mining maintained its lead as the most important industry. The annual gold production bounced upward to $70,000,000 in 1857, a level of production which lasted until the close of the decade.

In the face of such astounding growth in numbers and in material prosperity, Californians could ill afford to neglect what at best was an outmoded system of inland transportation. From state, local, and even federal sources came limited funds for road construction.

In 1855 the California legislature made available $100,000 for a road through Johnson's cut-off in the Sierra Nevada Mountains, another $20,000 for a road to go from San Pedro through Cajon Pass to the state boundary in the direction of the Mormon capital, and lesser sums to be expended in other parts of the state.

Private road and transportation companies, however, remained by far the heaviest contributors to road building during the 'fifties. With headquarters at Los Angeles the thriving freighting and staging firm of Alexander and Banning found it to their interest to keep the roads in passable shape for their fleet of wagons and coaches which served Salt Lake City, Fort Yuma, the mining districts on the Kern River, and local points in the environs of Los Angeles.

By 1858 there were sixty-four turnpikes in the state, and many of these were privately owned. At the close of the decade the California Stage Company, which had done much road building along its own routes of travel, boasted that (except for a twenty-mile pack trail over Trinity Mountain) the company could drive its coaches over a 700-mile stretch from Sacramento to Portland, Oregon.

There is little to be said in favor of the quality of California's roads at any time between 1848 and 1860. But from the point of view of miles of road constructed the people of the state are entitled to considerable praise. By 1860 practically all the towns in the state were connected by a network of passable roads. Sacramento remained the center from which roads radiated south to Mexico, north to Oregon, east to Nevada, and west to the Pacific Ocean. Cutting across these arterials were scores of important roads which were the avenues of communication between hundreds of widely scattered cities, towns, and farms of the state.

Together with the increase and spread of population and the construction of wagon roads went the development of the staging business. During 1854 and 1855 the California Stage Company exerted every effort to establish and maintain a monopoly of the staging business. But it was impossible to continue to do this indefinitely. At no time did the large firm crush all opposition, and by 1856 so many independent lines existed in the state that apparently about one-half of a total of approximately 3,000 miles of stage lines was controlled by rivals of the famous Sacramento firm.

The California Stage Company was, nevertheless, clearly the most important stagecoach company before 1860. It held the largest number of government mail contracts, and it was the only concern of its kind which served practically every settled area in the state.

Through the 'fifties the company pushed ahead. In 1856 James Haworth replaced President Birch, who thereafter set his cap for a federal overland-mail contract. Under the leadership of Haworth numerous projects were vigorously pushed. The road between Sacramento and Yreka was built through his efforts, in order that staging might be extended to the Siskiyou and Oregon communities and to such out-of-the-way places as Weaverville.

When the Sacramento Valley Railroad was completed in 1856, this same stage company was again the first to make arrangements for the transfer of passengers from California's first railroad train to stagecoaches at given points along the Sacramento-Folsom route.

The Sacramento Valley Railroad was a distinctly new and, to the Californians, a novel mode of travel between San Francisco and the northern mines. A description of a combined steamboat, railroad, and stagecoach journey is given in a letter dated April 26, 1856, from a miner to the editor of the *California Farmer:*

" . . . . I hasten to give you a sketch of my journey from San Francisco to this important mining locality [Nevada County]. After leaving our mutual friends at the Bay, I found myself on board one of the Steam Navigation's Company's fine boats, which are not surpassed by any. . . . .

"In the morning after my arrival in Sacramento City, I found myself comfortably seated in one of the railway cars, which for ease are perhaps equal to any I have yet seen, and I consider myself a competent judge. . . . . This line extends to a place called Folsom, and in the course of events will be further extended. . . . . After my arrival at Folsom, I placed myself in one of the California Stage Company's coaches, bound for my mountain home. I would recommend my friends who are troubled with dyspepsia, to take a trip in one of these coaches in the mountains, and I will guarantee that the jolting they will receive will be better than any physician's prescription; and can safely say that they will be effectually cured. . . . ."

From 1857 until the close of the decade the California Stage Company concentrated its activities in the northern rather than in the southern part of California. It made no extensions to its lines south of San Francisco; but in the north there was considerable progress. Shortly after the opening of railroad service between Sacramento and Folsom the California Stage Company transferred its headquarters from Sacramento to Marysville. New routes were soon opened in Klamath, Trinity, and Shasta counties; a saddle line between Yreka and French Gulch was purchased; a stagecoach expedition was fitted out to cross the Sierra by way of Honey Lake; and the Feather River line was extended from Oroville to Quincy.

In reviewing the development of the California Stage Company up to the autumn of 1858, the *Marysville Express* remarked that there were but few enterprises "equal in magnitude of operations, in amount of capital invested or number of men employed." The same account states that the company was then running twenty-eight daily stage lines, for which 1,000 horses, 134 Concord coaches and wagons, and 184 agents, drivers, and hostlers were employed. The total length of the routes was about 1,970 miles and involved more than 1,000,000 annual miles; and over more than 1,200 miles of the distance the California Stage Company carried the United States mail. In conclusion, the *Marysville Express* stated:

"The operations of the Company are necessarily diffused over a vast scope of territory; notwithstanding this, however, ... the business is centered in one office and under the immediate direction and control of one head, and is conducted with all the regularity and exactness characteristic of a banking house. . . . ."

By 1859 the Oregon Territory was sufficiently populous to apply for statehood; but, like the people of California, those of Oregon found themselves in a state of "unusual isolation." To ameliorate this condition the United States government granted a four-year (1860-1864) contract to the California Stage Company to carry mails between Sacramento and Portland, Oregon. Seven hundred and ten miles were thus added to the California Stage Company lines, which made this concern the second-largest staging company in the United States.

Stagecoach and mail service between California and Oregon was inaugurated on September 15, 1860. In the opinion of the *Sacramento Union,* it was the beginning of "an important era in the history of California staging. . . . ." The real value of this extension was that it did away with "the delays of the uncertain Ocean mail service."

The California Stage Company made no public statements; but, according to the *Union,* an "impression of the extent of their operations" may be obtained from the fact that from July 1859 to July 1860 the Sacramento agent alone contracted for 545 tons of barley and 467 tons of hay for the use of lines radiating from Sacramento. And although travel was "comparatively light" in 1860, the *Union* estimated that the receipts for one month over the Sacramento-Portland line would be $4,000.

The California Stage Company had disposed of its lines south of Sacramento by 1860, and only three principal centers remained —Sacramento, Folsom, and Marysville— from which stage lines radiated to points in northern California and Oregon. From Sacramento separate lines extended to Portland, Marysville, Auburn, Nevada City, Rattlesnake, Dutch Flat, Colusa, and Nevada City by way of Auburn. From Folsom transfers were made to all lines, and from Marysville stage lines extended to Yreka via Red Bluff and Shasta City, to Downieville via Foster's Bar, to Grass Valley and Nevada City, to Bidwell's Bar via Ophir, to Forbestown, and to Parks Bar.

In the summer of 1858 silver was discovered in large quantities in Nevada, not far from the trail over which immigrants passed en route to California. Unusually rich silver deposits, known in history as the Comstock Lode, were found in the spring of 1859; and the excitement following this discovery was not very different from that which had occurred in California ten years before.

These mining developments in the Utah Territory immediately affected the staging business in California. As a result of previous enterprises a passable road was prepared to accommodate the heavy traffic induced by the discovery of the Comstock Lode. Since these improvements had been sponsored by the Pioneer Line, then under the proprietorship of Louis McLane, the latter concern, and not the California Stage Company, reaped the greatest benefits from the trans-Sierra business.

Throughout the decade numerous "Opposition" lines held on and continued to give the big concern a run for its money; but through it all the California Stage Company maintained its leadership.

Meanwhile Wells, Fargo and Company had capitalized the advantages gained by the failure of the Adams concern in 1855. The Pacific Express—successor to Adams—had failed to recoup the proud position held by its predecessor. In fact, Wells, Fargo and Company outdistanced all its rivals in the number of express packages received at the port of San Francisco, in gold shipments, and in the number of express offices in the state. In 1856 the number of Wells Fargo offices in California was eighty, and by 1860 it was 147.

After 1855, Wells, Fargo and Company changed its personnel

as well as its organization, although it continued to be a joint stock company. At the beginning of 1856 its capital was placed, as in the previous year, at $600,000; but on November 17, 1859, the directors agreed to increase the capital stock by $1,000,000 with 10,000 new shares worth $100 each. And, finally, the life of the company was to be extended twenty years.

A notable boost was given to this concern when in 1856 important organization changes were made. Most fortunate of all the shifts made was the appointment of Louis McLane, formerly of the Pioneer Line, as general agent, with full authority in California. Under McLane's direction cash assets of the firm mounted steadily and, as we have already indicated, the scope and volume of business increased correspondingly.

Wells Fargo's financial statements for the period 1856 to 1860 show that the annual gross income from transportation increased from $251,400.85 to $430,293.41, and that the net income from express operations increased from $44,349.63 to $151,128.47. These figures show that without any question Wells Fargo was on a sound, profit-making basis by 1860. By then all threats from its competitors had faded, and in the public mind the magic name of Wells, Fargo and Company became synonymous with efficient service and successful business enterprise.

Chapter 8

THE BUTTERFIELD OVERLAND MAIL

O F COURSE MOST CALIFORNIANS wanted a railroad to the Pacific. But until it could be constructed, the immediate establishment of overland stage lines was demanded. The public was not content with the Pacific Mail Steamship Company, which, to the disgust of the people, offered at first only monthly service between the East and the West. Beginning in 1850, pleas for overland mail and passenger service were featured almost daily in the California newspapers. William M. Gwin and John C. Frémont, the state's first senators, likewise made it a matter of business to present in Congress resolutions and petitions with the same purpose in mind. To a country torn with sectional bickerings there was even added the threat of establishing a Pacific republic lest something be done about better, faster, and cheaper communication between the East and the West.

To its credit be it said that Washington was not unmindful of its obligations, and in Congressman R. H. Stanton Californians found a staunch friend. In his report on post offices and post roads, dated April 1850, Stanton recommended that improvements should be hastened. "California is far distant," he said, "and it appears to me that I am stating a self-evident proposition when I say that the government itself must either open a way to that distant land, or encourage its citizens so to do." He added: "The claim of the people of the West to have an immediate, safe, and practicable overland route, to serve until a railroad is built, I think a fair, reasonable, righteous, and a constitutional claim."

The great wheels of the federal government began turning—slowly and methodically—but for the growing West Coast giant they produced ant hills. For a youthful and active people—a group demanding speed and progress—the politics at Washington first produced a transportation system which even the ancient Persians would have scorned.

The first of these feeble steps to establish overland communication was taken by the federal government on April 25, 1851, when a contract was granted to Absalom Woodward and George Chorpenning to carry mails monthly between Sacramento and Salt Lake City. This new route was an extension of a similar line previously established by Samuel H. Woodson between Independence, Missouri, and the city of the Saints. The total time that would elapse in the transmission of mail between Sacramento and Salt Lake City would be thirty days, and an equal number of days would be allowed to cover the distance from the latter place to Independence, Missouri. Therefore two months would elapse between the time a letter was deposited in the post office in Sacramento before it was delivered in Missouri. An additional week would then be added for delivery along the Atlantic seaboard. Preposterous! but true!

It was a beginning in the right direction; but it was a really pathetic affair in the eyes of the West. No provision at all was made for passenger service; and because of inadequate equipment the transmission of the mails left much to be desired. The service was operated upon a schedule which permitted a single team to make the entire trip.

One cannot but admire the courage of these pioneer mail carriers, who, all alone in the Indian country, in all kinds of weather, trudged ever forward with their tired teams. They did the best they could under the circumstances, and people were grateful. Their effort to get the mails through on time, or at least through, is a saga of Western heroism and endurance for which blood and death were offered on the altar of public service. For all their shortcomings, these mail carriers were, after all, the first to provide somewhat regular overland-mail service between California and the East.

The South was in the saddle after the Mexican War, and it is not surprising that the next but likewise abortive effort in behalf of California became associated with the land of cotton and Long Horn cattle.

During 1849 a military express had been in operation over the famous old Santa Fe Trail, and during the following year the government established regular monthly stagecoach and mail service over this route. Santa Fe likewise became the beneficiary of another mail line which extended southward from Santa Fe to El Paso and thence southeastward to San Antonio. Mail service over this latter route was on a twenty-five day basis.

It was in this same extremely southern region that United States Postmaster General Aaron V. Brown established still another slow-moving postal route—this one to extend to California. Selecting San Antonio as the eastern terminal, he had the route overlap the Santa Fe–El Paso line as far as El Paso and proceed westward over prairie and sagebrush to San Diego. As one person phrased it, the line ran "from no place through nothing to nowhere." It was indeed difficult for Californians to anticipate much relief from it. It was June 1857 before the contract was let for the establishment of what was officially called the San Antonio and San Diego Mail. The award was made to none other than James Birch, who, after resigning as president of the California Stage Company, had gone to Washington seeking larger plums. The San Antonio and San Diego Mail would provide semi-monthly service on a thirty-day schedule. For this Birch would receive $150,000 per year in compensation from the government.

In less than thirty days, Birch, the capable veteran stageman, dispatched the first mail west from San Antonio. Mules, rather than horses, were used to pull the coaches; and for this reason, and probably also because pack mules actually carried the mails over the final 180-mile stretch from Fort Yuma to San Diego, Birch's new venture was known derisively as the "Jackass Mail."

It was easy for Californians to scorn the Jackass Mail; for, after all, they had reason to hope for something better. Yet as a feat of rapid improvisation the San Antonio and San Diego Mail is worthy of esteem. Moreover, it was Birch's last contribution to the furtherance of transportation in the West. Shortly after service had begun Birch drowned at sea. In him California lost a great pioneer, a successful entrepreneur, and a man much beloved by all who knew him and by thousands of others who knew him only as a prominent California stageman. Birch left behind his widow and a son who, as evidence of Birch's financial success, lived comfortably in a massive frame house at Swansea, Massachusetts. Later the widow married Frank S. Stevens, Birch's life-long pal and business associate.

Even though preparations were now under way for the establishment of the great Butterfield Overland Mail, service over the Jackass line continued and even improved during 1857-1858. Dates of departure from each end were the 9th and 24th of each month. The route, 1,476 miles long, was usually traversed in twenty-three days instead of the allotted thirty, and the record time was twenty-one days. A military convoy accompanied the mail through the treacherous Apache country, but even this was no positive insurance against Indian attack.

Following the death of Birch, the line was taken over by R. E. Doyle and George H. Giddings, and under their management through passenger service began in November 1857. In its advertisements the concern called attention to its new coaches, each drawn by six mules. Through 1857, however, there remained a 180-mile stretch on the western end, over which "we cross on mule back." Passengers were given provisions, "except where the Coach stops at Public Houses along the Line, at which each will pay for his own meal." The fare was $200. At best, though, there was little luxury on the Jackass line, and passengers often suffered great hardships.

Much of the usefulness of the San Antonio and San Diego Mail had come to an end when, in September 1858, operations of the Butterfield Overland Mail began. Thereafter Butterfield handled the Jackass line's business over a 600-mile stretch between El Paso and a point near San Diego. Even so, and contrary to all expectations, the San Antonio and San Diego Mail, so often the butt of Western jokes, held on until August 1861.

Operators of the pioneer overland lines are entitled to high praise. But all the goodwill in the world could not enable the Jackass line and others of its type to satisfy the transportation needs of California. Moreover, there were heartbreaking delays in the passage by Congress of a Pacific railroad act, which, more than anything else, the Californians wanted.

Exasperated Westerners in Congress began agitation, therefore, for faster and more frequent overland service between the East and San Francisco—not to some out-of-the-way place such

as San Diego. Early in 1856 no less than four bills with this end
in view were introduced in Congress. All these proposals failed, as
did also an amendment offered in August to the annual Post Office
Appropriations Bill which would have provided $500,000 for fast
semi-weekly service.

Each try came nearer to success. Finally, in February 1857, a
bill meeting the requirements came to the floor of Congress for
debate. Disagreements between the House and the Senate developed; but the differences were compromised in conference, and
on March 3, 1857, Congress passed, and the President subse-
quently approved, a Post Office Appropriations Bill which contained amendments designed to establish adequate overland mail
service.

A notice issued by Postmaster General Brown gave the provisions of the act, and those pertaining to the overland mail read
as follows:

"*Sec. 10.* That the Postmaster General be, and he is hereby,
authorized to contract for the conveyance of the entire letter mail
from such point on the Mississippi river as the contractors may
select to San Francisco, in the State of California, for six years, at
a cost not exceeding three hundred thousand dollars per annum for
semi-monthly, four hundred and fifty thousand dollars for weekly,
or six hundred thousand dollars for semi-weekly service, to be performed semi-monthly, weekly, or semi-weekly, at the option of the
Postmaster General.

"*Sec. 11.* That the contract shall require the service to be performed with good four-horse coaches or spring wagons, suitable
for the conveyance of passengers as well as the safety and security
of the mails.

"*Sec. 12.* And be it further enacted, That the contractors shall
have the right of preemption to three hundred and twenty acres of
any land not then disposed of or reserved, at each point necessary
for a station, not to be nearer than ten miles from each other; and
provided that no mineral land shall be thus preempted.

"*Sec. 13.* That the said service shall be performed within twenty-five days for each trip; ...."

This was it. This was the act the West had waited for, pending
railroad construction. This was the act James Birch had hoped
for, and under which he dreamed of operating a really gigantic

line of stages. At last there was joy in the Western camp, even though the whole measure was loaded with southern politics.

Two questions arose immediately. What route would be followed, and who would receive the contract to operate the stages? Postmaster General Brown, and he alone, held the key to the answers.

Few doubted that Brown would favor anything but a southern route; hence no one was very much surprised when he announced that "after full and mature consideration" the route would have two eastern terminals on the lower Mississippi: one, St. Louis; the other, Memphis, which was the Postmaster General's home town. The routes leading westward from the two places would converge at Fort Smith, Arkansas, and continue from there together. This western portion passed through Indian Territory to Colbert's Ferry, Texas, on the Red River, southwest across Texas to Franklin (opposite El Paso), west across southern New Mexico Territory to Fort Yuma, California, on the Colorado River, and thence "through the best passes . . . . to San Francisco."

The route as it was finally staked out within California dipped southward from Fort Yuma into Mexico, re-entered the state near the New River, and led to Los Angeles by way of Warner's Ranch. From this thriving southern city the route went north through the San Joaquin Valley to Fresno, thence over Pacheco Pass and through the towns of Gilroy and San Jose, and finally to the terminal city of San Francisco.

The total distance from St. Louis to San Francisco was officially measured at 2,757½ miles. The distance from the second eastern terminal of Memphis to Fort Smith, where the south fork joined the main line, was about 400 miles. First plans to use riverboat transportation over this section miscarried, and Butterfield was forced to make last-minute subleases with other stage companies over at least parts of the stretch.

Those not conversant with politics might have wondered why such a mammoth southern dip in the overland mail route was necessary. If people could think of no reason why this was, they at least had the satisfaction of knowing that when in operation this mail stage route would be the longest in the history of the world. Americans, then as now, loved to do things on a big scale.

Next, who would get the contract? Heading the group of suc-

A California stage company advertisement in the late 'fifties

Passenger train schedules to meet the stages

Stagecoach on a mountain road in California

cessful bidders was John Butterfield of New York, another self-made man, who had risen from stage driver to founder of the important American Express Company in 1850. He was well known to President James Buchanan, a fellow New Yorker. An approving nod from Buchanan doubtless influenced Postmaster General Brown in making the final decision in favor of Butterfield, whose associates included William G. Fargo and William B. Dinsmore. Also participating in the bid were J. V. P. Gardner, M. L. Kinyon, and other substantial persons representing New York interests.

Birch had been a strong competitor; but in the face of such a combination it is not surprising that the former president of the California Stage Company failed to secure the contract, especially since Brown was not obliged by law to award it to the lowest bidder.

The service to be provided would be on a semi-weekly basis, for which, as stated, the law would allow $600,000 annually for a period of six years. One year after the date of signing—September 16, 1858—service would begin. Many though the obstacles were, it was the Postmaster General's belief that, "looking at the respective bidders, both as to amount proposed and the ability, qualifications and experience," he had picked the right men to do the job.

Brown made no apologies for the long southern route. He said: "The Department supposed Congress to be in search of a route that could be found safe, comfortable, and certain during every season of the year." He believed that he had found such a route.

During the year of preparation there were many who said: "It's a speculation scheme," "They don't intend to carry it out," "It can't be done." Butterfield drew on long years of experience, and Fargo doubtless contributed wisdom.

Butterfield arranged for rail transportation from St. Louis to Tipton, the western rail terminal in Missouri, and organized this stretch into a special division. From Tipton to San Francisco the distance would be covered entirely by horse-drawn stages. The latter section he organized into eight separate divisions. At intervals, averaging about eighteen miles, he erected 139 stations. Building materials for these were whatever nature afforded; some were built of stone, some of adobe, and others of lumber. Wells were sunk at great cost and effort in desert areas. When no water was found, arrangements were made for hauling it to the required places. Coaches of various types were ordered for delivery before the opening day. A type of coach preferred for certain rough, mountainous stretches of the road was the "Celerity," or mud, wagon. Concords were much preferred over Troy coaches, but Butterfield could not be too "choosey." New and more luxurious coaches would come later. Horses and mules were acquired by the hundreds, and great quantities of hay and grain were bought to feed them. Most of the animals were mustangs rounded up on the range—"wild as deer, and as active as an antelope." Division managers, station attendants, hostlers, stage drivers, shotgun messengers, and other types of personnel were hired. It was a task truly worthy of the great business genius that was John Butterfield.

While the Butterfield concern struggled feverishly to meet the deadline, public interest in the project appears to have waned. Perhaps the rising tempo of the great political battle between the North and the South—Bleeding Kansas, the Dred Scott case, the Lincoln-Douglas debates, and the like—drew people's thoughts away from the still wild West.

When the deadline of September 16, 1858, approached, Butterfield was ready. Actually the eastbound stage left San Francisco one day ahead of schedule; but it was on the morning of the 16th, exactly one year after the date of contract, that the first mail marked "Per Overland Mail" started westward from St. Louis over the Butterfield route. There were but two bags of mail, and Butterfield personally attended to them. He accompanied this shipment on the train as far west as Tipton, where mail from the Memphis line would be added.

The only through passenger on the westbound journey was Waterman L. Ormsby, twenty-one-year-old special correspondent for the *New York Herald*. Ormsby made the trip as a representative of his newspaper and wrote six very good and interesting articles about his experiences.

There was one thing that surprised Ormsby about the take-off both from the train depot at St. Louis and from the stage terminal at Tipton, and this was the absence of public demonstration. When the first stage left Tipton on this historic drive across the West, "Not a cheer was raised" from the party gathered there. "Had they been wild Indians they could not have exhibited less emotion."

The coach in which Ormsby rode was described as sturdy. The body rested on thorough-braces and had a top made of canvas. It had three seats, the backs of which could be let down to form one bed for four to ten people "according to their size and how they lie."

Travel was, of course, continued day and night, with the usual brief stops for change of four-horse teams and for meals. The road through the Ozarks of southwestern Missouri was very dusty and stony, and in places the hills were steep and rugged.

For the first three days Ormsby went without sleep. "It took some time to get accustomed to the jolting over the rough road, the rocks, and log bridges," but by the end of the third day he was "quite oblivious" to these discomfitures of stagecoach travel.

Through Indian Territory no warm meals were served. Butterfield had been thoughtful enough to provide a basket of food along with "the needful with which to wash it down," and not until this supply had been exhausted did he comment on the homely meals provided between Fort Tipton and Fort Smith. Twelve days out, near El Paso, Texas, the westbound overland stage met the one eastbound from San Francisco. Down through the lonely prairie country much remained to be done by way of completing stations, and the building of additional ones. No Indian troubles were experienced, and the weather was fine. One handicap for many of the drivers was the newness of the road. Some got lost, others failed to gauge the time correctly while making their respective runs.

At other times mules, some of them caught and harnessed for the first time, others "stubborn and lazy," would throw the most diligent jehu off schedule. At one place the temperamental behavior of the mule team caused a delay of several hours. Whether it was the driver's fault, an act of Providence, just plain mule balkiness, or a combination of all these, Ormsby did not say. As a good reporter he simply recorded that the "mules reared, pitched, twisted, whirled, wheeled, ran, stood still, and cut up all sorts of capers. The wagon performed so many evolutions that I, in fear of my life, abandoned it and took to my heels, fully confident that

I could make more progress in a straight line, with much less risk of breaking my neck."

Through western Arizona and California the stage traveled old and familiar roads and there was less uncertainty about holding to a schedule. And west of Tucson whom should Ormsby meet as assistant or sub-superintendent but our old friend and veteran stageman, Warren F. Hall. The correspondent described Hall as "a man of much energy" who "soon sets matters straight." It had been Hall who had stocked the line between Tucson and Los Angeles, and in Ormsby's opinion some of the finest horses were used over this stretch.

Hall personally drove. It was over a good but none-the-less precarious road that led ultimately to San Diego. To Ormsby this part was fascinating. He was impressed by odd terrain and the massive desert-plant life, not to mention Hall's skill as a driver. His impression concerning the scenery was definitely not shared by another who thought the journey rather dull and declared that "if God ever pronounced this part of the earth good, it was more than ever man did."

Warner's Ranch made a pleasant impression upon the youthful New York correspondent, and from this place on he had the feeling of getting into civilization again and on to the home stretch. At Chino Ranch he was in the heart of California's rich cattle country; but he noted the absence of milk and butter at breakfast, "without which the merest hod carrier in New York would think a meal incomplete."

Los Angeles County was truly a land of "The Angels" because of the richness of its soil. Ormsby described the city of Los Angeles as having 6,000 inhabitants, mostly Mexicans and Indians, and said that the city had a number of "fine buildings." He commented upon the thrifty and business-like character of the city; and what must have looked inviting to any stagecoach passenger from across the desert were the vineyards heavily loaded with "luscious grapes," and the premium fruits that were grown there.

The drive through the San Joaquin Valley elicited little comment. Between Pacheco Pass and Gilroy some of the fastest driving of the entire trip was experienced. Ormsby was in the box with the jehu who was intent upon getting through in good time.

"It's best to keep the wheels rolling, or they'll slide," said the driver to Ormsby, when asked to apply the brakes while going down the steepest hill at top speed. "The loosening of a nut, the breaking of a strap, the shying of one of the four spirited horses, might—indeed would—have sent us all to 'kingdom come' without a chance for saying prayers! But just as I made such a reflection, crack went the whip and away we flew, at a rate I know would have made old John Butterfield, the president of the mail company, and a very experienced stage man, wish himself safely home," wrote Ormsby.

The time actually made was twelve miles in one hour and five minutes.

Now at last the home stretch had been reached. People gathered at Gilroy to see the stage come in, and Ormsby was flooded with questions about the East and about the trip.

Santa Clara Valley looked beautiful with its orchards laden with fruit. San Jose was reached at one o'clock in the morning of October 10th, and, according to the *San Jose Telegraph,* the sleepy citizens of this city of 3,000 were merely aroused by the "unusual noise at such an hour."

The remaining fifty miles to the end of the trail were made during the darkest hours of night; but at sunrise the city of San Francisco "hove in sight over the hills, and never did the night traveller approach a distant light, or the lonely mariner descry a sail, with more joy than did I the city of San Francisco on the morning of Sunday, October 10. As we neared the city we met milkmen and pleasure seekers taking their morning rides, looking on with wonderment as we rattled along at a tearing pace."

Dashing over pavement stones, the coach soon reached the Plaza. From the driver's horn came a shrill blast to signalize the safe arrival of the first United States Mail over the Butterfield Overland.

The time was seven-thirty o'clock, just twenty-three days, twenty-three hours and a half since Ormsby and those two mail bags had set out from St. Louis. The time required in the contract, it is recalled, was "within twenty-five days." The average rate of speed had been a little less than five miles per hour. The slowest time, an average of two and one-half miles per hour, had been made between El Paso and Tucson; the fastest average was seven and one-half miles, made through California. Ormsby praised the employees of the company for their courtesy, ability, and devotion to duty. On the whole, therefore, the Butterfield Overland Mail was a success; above all, it was an accomplished fact.

Only a few of those traveling the Butterfield line left such complete records of their experiences as did Ormsby. Others comparable with it came from the pens of G. Bailey, special agent for the Post Office Department, J. M. Farwell, correspondent of the San Francisco *Alta California,* and William Tallack, an English traveler.

Bailey accompanied the first mail eastward from San Francisco. In an official report to Postmaster General Brown he also had much to praise about the Butterfield venture. "I feel safe in expressing the opinion," he wrote, "that a continued exertion of the energy and perseverance which have thus far characterized the operations of the Overland Mail Company, will enable the contractors to reduce the time to twenty days." He seemed very much impressed that the company had overcome amazing obstacles, such as scarcity of water over "long sand deserts," and building and maintaining stations hundreds of miles from points of supply; but he said they had yet to cope with the hostile Apaches and Comanches at whose mercy they were operating.

Conflict with the Indians was not long in coming. Farwell saw trouble brewing when making the trip in October 1858. In the San Simon's Valley this incident was reported. Some Apache braves approached a stage conductor and their leader, Mangus Colorado, demanded some corn. The conductor, an old Indian fighter, said he had no corn. This was a lie, as the braves soon discovered by prowling around the wagons at the station. When Mangus Colorado learned that he had been deceived, he went back to the conductor and blurted out: "Want twelve sacas corn damn quick." Observing the approach of seventy-five or eighty other Apaches, the conductor delivered the corn "damn quick." Still other Indian scares came near El Paso.

The Englishman Tallack, who made the West-to-East trek in 1860, appears to have been more impressed by the landscape than by human factors. He could not, however, resist commenting on the "tough beefsteak" breakfasts at four in the morning in a "dirty, dusty adobe," upon the frequency of murders ("private assassination") along the trail, upon the ominous presence of Indians, and upon the "solemn, silent loneliness" of the prairies. Like most passengers, Tallack made it through without bodily harm; and like most others who traveled the Butterfield Overland Mail, he accepted this rough-and-tumble mode of travel with good grace.

As a matter of fact, the line appears to have gained steadily in public favor, and in 1860 it handled more mail than did the ocean steamers. Efforts made to cancel the contract in favor of a more northerly route did not succeed until the Civil War made such a move imperative.

Chapter 9

"MOCHILA" MAIL

LL DAY SUNDAY AND MONDAY, March 18 and 19, 1860, the St. George Hotel in Sacramento was besieged by a congregation of about 200 toughened, eager young horsemen. They were the type that could have been found only in California, where every native was at home on a horse. It looked like a rodeo. On the streets was exhibited the finest horseflesh, adorned with the most elaborate silver work and saddle art. Riders vied in relating exploits, for each hoped to discourage the others among the applicants who had responded with surprising enthusiasm to Agent William Finney's advertisement for "ten or a dozen men . . . . as hostlers or riders on the Overland Express Route via Salt Lake City," starting wages offered for station attendants being "$50 per month and found." Post riders were to be given from $100 to $150, with extra pay for longer runs. Often during the anxious days of the Civil War, California merchants made up a bonus to be divided among the riders for extra-fast delivery, cutting scheduled time by minutes, hours, and even days.

For a month or more the West had been agog with the rumor, soon confirmed, that Russell, Majors and Waddell, the famous freighting and staging concern of the plains, planned a fast overland mail via the central route. Finally, California, the Cinderella stepchild, was to have a really fast mail service. Nine days to the East, think of it! What's more, it was said on good authority that in the East dashing William H. Russell had wagered $200,000 (conservatives said $10,000) that this feat would be performed. Nothing small about Mr. Russell! You may be certain, too, that

120

considerable private and public betting was done by boosters and cynics in all parts of the West.

On February 29 the *San Francisco Bulletin* announced that Russell, Majors and Waddell had decided to start a Pony Express between St. Joseph, Missouri, and Placerville, California, on the third of April. The cost for through letter service would be five dollars in gold for every half ounce, with rates for shorter distances prorated. "Their object in establishing this express is not so much to make money at present as it is to prove by actual experiment the superiority of the Salt Lake route," properly acknowledged the *Sacramento Union* in boosting the new venture.

Presently the schedule was announced. Telegraphic dispatches would be received until 3:45 each Tuesday afternoon. These messages would be sent from Sacramento in nine days to St. Joseph in a glorious horseback relay, then telegraphed to the East coast. Letters would take but thirteen days.

Until stations could be built at points between Sacramento and the Carson Valley, tent shelters for horses and men were to be erected each twelve or fifteen miles. Farther on, the distance between stops was often more than twenty-five miles. At each station the rider would be allowed but two minutes to transfer his precious cargo to a fresh mount. Ordinarily each horseman would ride three horses to make up his stint.

All of the riders chosen were small but sinewy; probably none weighed over 135 pounds and many little more than 100. Every possible step was taken to save weight. Saddles were specially designed, hybrids of the "Western" and jockey types—lightweight with saddle horns and cantles for comfort in riding those long distances. They were only about a third the weight of the saddles of the *vaqueros,* the types then commonly used in California. Even the stirrups and tapaderas were lighter than ordinary. Most of these saddles were made by Israel Landis' famous saddlery in St. Louis.

No details were overlooked in making the elaborate preparations. Peculiar to the Pony Express was its interesting *mochila,* or leather blanket, thrown over the saddle, with holes for the horn and cantle. Ordinary mail pouches—those used for regular mail— were much too awkward and cumbersome and so were not to be used in the new service. Specially designed *mochilas,* adapted from the Spanish, were made with four *cantinas,* locked pockets of hard leather, fastened to the *mochila* and lined with oilskin to protect the precious mail from the sweat of the beast, from the rain and snow, or from swollen streams, should the rider be forced to swim his horse. As not more than twenty pounds could be carried, tissue-thin paper was used for the letters. Often the cargo weighed only ten or fifteen pounds. The envelopes were handstamped until the Wells Fargo interests took charge in May 1861. As the rider straddled the horse, there was a pocket in front of and behind each thigh. Only the agents at either end of the line and specially designated officials had keys to these locked pockets, but the "way" pocket was left open for messages taken or delivered along the route and for the waybill on which the name of the station and the time of arrival and departure were to be noted.

In actual operations the riders performed their acts with the skill of modern circus riders. Because of the ease of switching the *mochila* at each station, it was possible to have the relief mount saddled and chafing at the bit to continue the run. Seldom did it take the two minutes allowed to make the change, and riders would often toss the *mochila* on the remount and swing from one saddle to the other with both ponies at a gallop, never touching the ground while making the change.

The distance regularly covered by a Pony expressman ranged from thirty-five to seventy-five miles, depending on the terrain he covered. The speed for the 1,966 miles—come hell or high water —had to average nine miles an hour. Some riders averaged twenty miles per hour; but delays caused by blizzards, torrential rains, excessive darkness, exhausting summer heat, and unforeseen accidents usually reduced the overall average to the scheduled figure. When the post rider reached the relief station, he rested till the next messenger dashed in from the opposite direction, then threw the leather *mochila* over his impatient horse, and returned to his "home" base. At first he made the round trip once a week, but it was not long until service was offered twice weekly.

In those days the aim of many an American boy was to be a Pony Express rider. In all, the number first assigned to this dangerous, but highly exciting, job was eighty. They were the pick of the crop, boys in their teens, dependable, strong, wiry, brave, and, as we have noted, astonishingly agile and accomplished horsemen. What they lacked in years they made up for in sheer nerve and physical stamina. Even so, few of these riders were able to stand the incessant pounding, pounding, pounding on the trail.

Let us return to that day of April 3, 1860. All was in readiness —the horses, the riders, the stations, and the nation. The Pony, as it was affectionately called, would leave San Francisco promptly at 4:00 P.M. on the fast river steamer, *Antelope,* for Sacramento. For San Francisco the occasion was an important one. Crowds gathered around the office of the Alta Telegraph Company where a "little nankeen-colored pony" waited all afternoon decked out with two little flags on his headstalls and mail bags impressively labeled "Overland Pony Express." Since Sacramento was the official western terminal, this was the only pony ever to leave San Francisco on the big run. The departure from the Bay city this first time was merely an advertising stunt in celebration of the big event.

At four o'clock sharp, Jim Randall, handsomely dressed for the occasion, leaped on the horse, dashed to the wharf and boarded the *Antelope* for Sacramento. Here William ("Billy") Hamilton truly initiated the service; but since it was then 2:45 A.M. no crowd was assembled.

As soon as the boat docked, the local mail was added, the *mochila* was thrown over the saddle, and the first official lap of the long relay began: to Placerville, over the towering Sierra, via Genoa to Carson City, Nevada. From this mining town the Pony followed Simpson's route through Fort Churchill, Ruby Valley, and Camp Floyd, and skirted the south end of Great Salt Lake to the Mormon capital. The scheduled time to Salt Lake was three and one-half days. Eastward to Fort Bridger, through South Pass to Fort Laramie, past Chimney Rock to old Julesburg, and along the Platte River raced the relay, over sandhills and prairies, to the Missouri River. At St. Joseph the mail would be put aboard a "fast" train for New York, and four days later it would be in the hands of those to whom it was directed. Arrangements were made with agents at either end of the East and West telegraph lines for immediate transmission of telegraphic messages.

In less than four hours the forty-five miles upgrade to Placerville were covered, and at this station the last letter was added to the way pocket, making a total of fifty-six letters from San Francisco, thirteen from Sacramento, and one from Hangtown (Placerville). Three hundred and fifty dollars were the meager receipts on the initial run.

The ride across the Sierra Nevada to Carson City was viewed with misgivings, because snow had been falling steadily in that region for several days. Drifts were thirty feet deep in places, people said. The Marysville stage had missed its first trip in three years.

The lad assigned to this dangerous run was Warren Upson. Upson was just a youth, but he had a man's experience in riding, shooting, prospecting, and exploring the Sierra region. The dangerous, exciting outdoor life was to his taste; and as soon as the announcement was made of the Pony Express he had applied to division superintendent, Bolivar Roberts, for a job as rider. The mount Upson had chosen for this first dash was a sure-footed, sturdy pony, not so speedy as Hamilton's but a sensitive and fearless animal that would sense a safe way if there was one.

When his moment came, Upson galloped off from Sportsman's Hall in Placerville, each of the watching men bidding him "Godspeed." The trail to Strawberry grew more and more hazardous. Landmarks were obscured by the snow. Thank Heaven, Roberts had insisted on this stretch being made in daylight. At places there were avalanches and—at least so it seemed to the rider—it was nip and tuck to get out of their way. At Hope Valley a fresh mount waited, and the wet, cold *mochila* shifted to the new mount. Seconds were saved by eager hands and words of encouragement were given for the tough trail ahead. Twenty-one miles farther on an eager remount waited at Woodbridge. On then to Genoa at a faster clip, for the snow was now behind them. Late at night Upson arrived at the Carson City home station after eighty-five miles of battling with the elements. Roberts would not be disappointed in his choice for this ride!

Now a cheer for the next rider. Remember, "The mail has got to go through." A pot of coffee simmering on the stove, plenty of food, admiring comments of folks gathered at the station— this was Upson's welcome. Predictions of the future of the Pony Express, questions about the sendoff in San Francisco and the hazards of the route just covered followed thick and fast. At last the curious group broke up to give the hero opportunity for a well-deserved rest.

Between Carson City and Camp Floyd three adobe shelters had been erected. This was a lonely stretch over a maze of ridges on a new trail opened by Captain Simpson and cutting off more than one hundred miles from Chorpenning's old route. The largest town between Missouri and California was Salt Lake City, and it was generally agreed that half the battle was won if the couriers from the East and West arrived there within the schedule time. So on to Salt Lake sprinted the Pony. Major Howard Egan, who had laid out the trail across the wastes of Utah and Nevada, personally rode with the mail from Rush Valley, Utah, to Salt Lake City on the first run, in scheduled time. Egan had already played a vital role as superintendent of the line from Salt Lake City to Carson City by selecting the best horses and men for the run. Among the riders were his own sons, Howard and Erastus.

Meanwhile there was also great enthusiasm in "St. Joe" over the commencement of the new service. Feverishly for several weeks William H. Russell and Alexander Majors had been engaged in hiring riders and in making innumerable arrangements to assure the success of this great venture. Nothing was too good for the boys. At this eastern terminal they were put up at the Patee House, "the finest hotel in the West," and dances were given in their honor. Plenty of color was provided by red shirts, blue trousers, fancy boots, and buckskin jackets. Of course, the men added their own trappings for the show in town; but on the route they would revert to the simplest, sturdiest dress and equipment. Jack H. Keetley, the "joyous jockey" who operated on the route out of St. Joe, later recalled that riders always rode out of town in full regalia but would leave their fine trappings on the ferry that carried them across the river. (In payment of a bet, Keetley once rode 340 miles without rest.) He claimed that Alex Carlisle was the first to carry the mail out of St. Joe, though claims are registered for several others.

At St. Joe an excited crowd had gathered to witness the first departure of the westbound Pony. Some pulled hairs from the tail of the "fine bay mare" to save and even sell as mementos of the great event. Jeff Thompson, the mayor, participated in the celebration and read a telegram of congratulations from President

Buchanan. The proud Russell was very much in evidence. A cannon boomed the signal for the start; the mail was locked in the *cantinas;* and off dashed the rider to the ferry *Denver,* proceeded from Elwood to Granada, where Don Rising threw the *mochila* over his pony, and so westward across the continent flew the Pony in its race against time.

It was the seventy-first horse of the relay team that dashed into Placerville at 2:30 P.M. on April 13. The *Sacramento Union* received the news by telegraph and hurriedly printed in its evening paper: "The fact of crossing on the Central route . . . . in nine days, has been accomplished by the Pony Express." The *Union* urged the population to welcome the Pony and escort him to the city. The result of the experiment showed that the proprietors had made perfect arrangements. To them "California is under deep obligations. In this Pony Express business they have illustrated the true spirit of progress," wrote the happy editor.

And Sacramento indeed welcomed the Pony. Both houses of the state legislature adjourned in order to welcome it. When the citizens heard that the rider was expected, the town was hastily decorated. Flags were flown from buildings and even stretched across the street. Impromptu window displays were got up. One place, a crockery store, had a hobby horse with the amusing inscription, "PONY EXPRESS. RUSSELL, MAJORS & CO. TAKE THE SKATES!" Another mounted a large doll on a wooden pony and stuffed letters and papers in its hand. Banners of brown paper, with mottoes hurriedly splashed. Nearly a hundred citizens and the local armed guard gathered along the road to await the Express.

In town the streets were milling with people. Ladies who were fortunate enough to get places on the balconies or in windows eagerly craned their necks for the first sight, ready to cheer and salute the hero. Men stood around in the April sun on rooftops animatedly discussing the enviable achievement.

At last an electric charge of excitement startled the crowd, and the cheering and pushing began, as one of the welcoming committee dashed into town at 5:25 P.M., harbinger of the approaching Pony. Bells rang out from church steeples and fire stations in all parts of the city. On the square at Tenth Street the boys of Young America, No. 6, fired the cannon nine times as a climax of their days of anticipation. Young America, No. 2, answered with a noisy shot from another piece of antiquated artillery, and their elders fired volleys from other stands. "Amidst the firing and shouting, and waving of hats and ladies' handkerchiefs, the pony—the veritable pony—was seen coming at a rattling pace down J street, surrounded by about thirty of the citizen deputation. . . . . A thick cloud of dust rolled over the heads of the party as it came dashing on in the most hopeless confusion. Such a scene— both for comicality and becoming enthusiasm—our city has never, perhaps, witnessed." So reported the *Union* the next day.

Out of the excited crowd emerged the rider, again Hamilton, who had carried the first *mochila* mail to French Butte. Six letters were hastily sorted out for Sacramento recipients, and the *mochila* was thrown on the back of the proxy pony destined to receive in San Francisco the tribute due the seventy-four others who should have shared directly in this glory.

While the steamer *Antelope* idled at the dock waiting for the Pony, San Francisco was informed by telegraph of its arrival in Sacramento. A fitting welcome was at once arranged. At the theaters the announcement was made that there would be a cere- monious reception when the boat landed, the Pony Express had proved to be a success and merited a real welcome. While the crowd built bonfires up the river and routed out the fire depart- ment to join the parade, the police, who could have done little to subdue the excitement, winked at the disturbance of the peace and joined the gala crowd. An eighteen-piece band wandered over the city waking the good folk who had hastened home to comparative quiet. Bacchus aided the revelry, while torches lighted up the water front with an almost terrifying glare, reminiscent of the numerous destructive fires. By midnight a hilarious crowd was listening to "Yankee Doodle" and other popular band numbers while young and old joined in impromptu dances on the wharves.

At 1:00 A.M. the steamer made fast, and the confused Pony, mounted by the bowing and smiling rider, trotted ashore. The pro- cession escorted the Pony to the Montgomery Street office of the C.O.C.&P.P. Express. The band led the procession, the fire engines fell in, and next came the vaunted Pony with the citizenry close on his heels. One admiring lady tied her bonnet ribbons about his neck. As the crowd gathered round, letters were distributed and numerous speeches were made, though probably few heard them in the hubbub.

Thus was scored a notable triumph. Despite financial headaches, improvement and maintenance work continued in the same spirit that had thus far been displayed. New shelters were constructed. Some of the shelters were miniature stockades, sixty feet square with eight- to ten-foot walls. Many had portholes through which men could sight and fire, and after Indian trouble started in 1860 they were often invaluable. The regular "home" stations were more comfortable. More men staffed these stops—extra riders, blacksmiths to shoe the spirited ponies, mule drivers for the overland stage, bullwhackers for the freighters, and visitors. Sometimes homesteaders or hostlers in tiny communities made extra money boarding riders and attendants and caring for the livestock.

It was fortunate that the freighting concern had set up frequent, well-stocked stops, because livestock had to be strictly guarded against thieving Indians and whites. Station tenders in these out-of-the-way places experienced a rough, dangerous, lonely life and because of it deserve little less recognition than the riders themselves. In fact, the number of casualties among station keepers from Indian depredations and road agents was greater than among riders. Many times a rider came into a station, his lathered steed gasping for relief, only to find the attendants massacred and the stock driven off or slaughtered. With not a second to spare, off the rider would go to warn the next stage and Pony station of impending danger.

There was plenty of Indian trouble. While Nick Wilson was waiting for the return mail at Pete Neece's Willow Springs, Nevada, station, Indians attacked—"the whole band of them yelling like a pack of demons." The men hid some distance from the station and fired at the redskins from all sides, scaring them off. In Spring Valley, two boys whose parents had died of cholera were left alone to care for the stock. They had to be quick and plucky lads to face Indian dangers alone. A daylight raid on the Mountain Springs station surprised John Applegate, Ralph Rosier, and Bolly Bolwinkle. Si McCandless, a squaw man, saved the day; but numerous stations were ravaged before these men brought the warning. Never a dull moment on the Pony trail!

The Pony Express (reproduced from A. L. Stimson,
History of the Express Business)

Overland stage along the central route during the 'sixties (reproduced
from A. L. Stimson, *History of the Express Business*)

Remains of the Colfax–Grass Valley stage

Courtesy of Donald Bates, Portland, Oregon

Ben Holladay, the stagecoach king

From the brittle, faded sheets of newspapers published in towns along the route come the few reports that bring to light the real valor of these horsemen. Some of the most dramatic episodes of the Pony Express tell of the supreme sacrifices made by the riders. In Nevada in 1860 a pony galloped into a way station with the rider slumped over the horn, his lifeless body pierced by several arrows. So tight was the clutch of his hand that the mane had to be cut from his grasp. The gallant pony had carried on, bringing the mail through safely. "Pony Bob" Haslam carrying the news of Lincoln's election was attacked, but reached his relief station after a remarkable ride of 120 miles in eight hours, his shattered jaw pierced by an arrow and his left arm badly wounded. Shortly after this experience this intrepid rider was back on the trail, ready to add new laurels to the Pony Express.

Little did these lads realize the demands upon their courage. Sometimes the overtaxed riders came into the homestretch with blood streaming from nose and mouth. Even so, many lived on to a ripe and reminiscent old age. Billy Fisher, one of the boys who helped carry the first *mochila* mail, was one of them. He retired to southeastern Idaho, where to new generations of adventurous Americans he told his vivid tales of narrow escapes from the "Injuns" and the elements. In conclusion, though, Billy would say it wasn't especially exciting:

". . . . it was all in the day's work. . . . . We just took things as they came." Howard Driggs, a recent chronicler of the Pony Express, found Charley Cliff, at nearly eighty, sparkling and eager to talk about the days when he sped the sixty miles from St. Joseph to Seneca, Kansas. Charley insisted it was Johnny Frey who carried the first mail West, despite the news account. "I ought to know," he insisted. "I was right there. . . . . He rode another mare called 'Sylph,' I believe. She was a little sorrel animal with four stocking feet."

A rider seldom carried any weapon but a bowie knife, sometimes a Colt's revolver or a rifle slung behind the shoulders; for the most part they depended on the fleet-footed ponies. Once on the plains "Pony Bob" was waylaid in a sheltering woods by Indians who were curious to see what this modern Pegasus carried that demanded such speed. Coming upon the ambush, Haslam spurred his horse and with a bloodcurdling whoop dashed through the middle of the "braves," defeating the very purpose for which they had gathered.

The legend of William ("Buffalo Bill") Cody, as a lad in his teens (fact and fiction alike fantastic), tells of his encounter with a highwayman while riding express. From the roadside the armed, masked figure stepped out. "I don't want to hurt you, boy, but I do want them bags," he suggested, flourishing his gun. When the desperado advanced to remove the *mochila*, Bill, unarmed, hands above his head, spurred his horse into the surprised victim, injuring him and making his capture simple. Towing his quarry into the station, Bill apologized to Mr. Christman for being a few minutes behind schedule!

Nick Wilson, whose story is told in *The White Indian Boy,* had a store of tales, not imaginative, but real experiences, to hold favored listeners spellbound. Without the horses there wouldn't have been any express, he claimed, and he heaped glory on them —heroes like Black Billy, who always brought the mail home, once bleeding and frothing, one arrow piercing his shoulder, another his flank. Then there was the impetuous, gray American Boy, which broke away while the mail was being switched, and streaked clear through the next station with the mail—riderless. While riding Nigger in Indian infested country, in what is now Nevada, Nick had to run the gantlet of an ambush. "I looked back over my shoulder and saw them comin'—about thirteen of the devils, as hard as they could right in after me, yellin' and shootin'. But Nigger's grain-fed muscles soon got me out of the danger of their arrows and the few old guns they had. Their grass-fed ponies couldn't keep long within gunshot."

It is significant that in all the mails carried by Pony Express only one pouch was lost. In another case, the rider was waylaid and murdered, but the mail was found and promptly delivered. No wonder the eyes of the entire nation were upon the Pony, and newspapers the country over headed the latest flashes "Via Pony Express." Abroad, too, its fame spread. J. Ross Browne in his *Adventures* says: "During my sojourn in Germany I received a letter from California by Pony Express in less than four weeks after it was written; and it was not until I showed the date and express stamp and carefully explained the whole matter that I was enabled to overcome the incredulity of my Teutonic friends."

Europeans soon found the service valuable. During the war between Britain and China some of Britain's official mail saved days by going across the West by Pony Express and then by clipper ship to the Orient. Some single communications cost as much as $135; naturally, few personal letters were carried.

Travelers across the plains watched for the lone rider, and the classic description of the brief glimpse of this poetry in action is caught by Mark Twain in *Roughing It*:

"We had a consuming desire, from the beginning, to see a pony-rider, but somehow or other all that passed us and all that met us managed to streak by in the night, so we heard only a whiz and a hail, and the swift phantom of the desert was gone before we could get our heads out of the windows. But now we were expecting one along every moment, and would see him in broad daylight. Presently the driver exclaims:

"'HERE HE COMES!'

"Every neck is stretched further and every eye strained wider. Away across the endless dead level of the prairie a black speck appears against the sky, and it is plain that it moves. Well, I should think so! In a second or two it becomes a horse and rider, rising and falling, rising and falling—sweeping toward us nearer and nearer—growing more and more distinct, more and more sharply defined—nearer and still nearer, and the flutter of the hoofs comes faintly to the ear—another instant a whoop and a harrah from our upper deck, a wave of the rider's hand, but no reply, and man and horse burst past our excited faces and go swinging away like a belated fragment of a storm!

"So sudden is it all, and so like a flash of unreal fancy, that but for the flake of white foam left quivering and perishing on a mail-sack after the vision had flashed by and disappeared, we might have doubted whether we had seen any actual horse and man at all, maybe."

The story behind this epic in transportation history is one of strange coincidence. In the fall of 1854, when William M. Gwin was traveling overland to resume his duties in Washington as Senator from California, he had for a companion B. F. Ficklin, general superintendent of Russell, Majors and Waddell's freighting concern. The men rode horseback by way of Sacramento, Salt Lake, South Pass, and down the Platte to St. Joseph, the very route they were both enthusiastically to support for the overland mail. These two roundly criticized the United States mail service in the West, and Gwin heatedly promised to use his newly acquired political influence to bring about some improvement. As a result of this conversation, Ficklin proposed the scheme for a chain of riders, according to Gwin.

True, there had been pony expresses before. Ancient Persian kings had a pony express, as had also Genghis Khan, the terrible Asiatic warrior of the twelfth and thirteenth centuries. And even in early Spanish California mounted soldier couriers were used to carry official mail between Mexican Loreto in Lower California and distant Monterey in Alta California. During the 'fifties, as we have already seen, California express companies had horseback messengers who met the steamers in San Pedro, San Francisco, and other port towns, carrying mail and special news to and from the more important mines and inland communities. In 1858 a most remarkable ride had been made by the sensational rider, F. X. Aubery—many are still incredulous—from Santa Fe to Independence, 800 miles, in five days and thirteen hours, without rest; but then, he had done it as a bit of showmanship and not as a business venture.

Almost immediately after Gwin's arrival in Washington he introduced a bill to establish a weekly mail between St. Louis and San Francisco, the time to be ten days and the remuneration $5,000 the round trip. The bill was pigeonholed in the Committee on Military Affairs. But when the Union was threatened and pressure increased from the West, which cited the excellent rail communications and magnetic telegraph service in the East, interest in the movement for speedier mail service to the Pacific revived. It was openly admitted that certain Western leaders were threatening to set up an independent Pacific Republic, so bitter were they about their isolation.

Never had anything of the magnitude of the Overland Pony Express in speed and regularity been propounded. If this experiment should prove successful, surely Washington could not ignore the proof that the central route was more practicable than the roundabout Butterfield route.

Record service over the Pacific Steamship Line was twenty-two days from New York to San Francisco, and Butterfield's best service across the southern desert wastes was twenty-one days. Gwin's proposal would reduce both more than half. Russell met Senator Gwin in Washington to discuss the idea and they formulated a plan. Confidently Russell guaranteed that his firm could and would establish such a Pony Express, and Gwin optimistically pledged that he would obtain a subsidy from Congress as soon as the express proved workable.

Only a firm with the immense assets and transportation experience of Russell, Majors and Waddell, which already was carrying mail on the plains, would be likely to sponsor such a scheme. Horace Greeley had written in 1859: "I presume this great firm has at this hour two millions of dollars invested in stock, mainly oxen, mules and wagons."

Even so, before the project was well under way, doubts of its financial success arose. When receipts failed even to approximate the heavy expenses, creditors stepped in and reorganization was effected. In 1861 Congress appropriated $1,000,000 to support jointly daily central overland stagecoach mail and semiweekly pony service. The Pony Express was to continue until completion of the transcontinental telegraph line.

The success of the first Pony run was the spur for the completion of this telegraph line from the foot of the Sierra Nevada to Missouri. On April 20, 1861, the Pony carried 260 letters out of San Francisco. Already the telegraph line was setting poles to Miller's station beyond Carson City, and by May 11 the time had been shortened three hours. Late in May the California legislature appropriated $100,000 for the construction of a telegraph line to the Mississippi Valley. Little did California realize the portentous developments in the East and the part the Pony was to play in holding the loyalty of California with the Union during the impending conflict.

All during the eighteen months' existence of the Pony Express the telegraph line was building. Closer and closer the terminals approached each other, and faster and faster raced the ponies. The record trip was made for the delivery of Lincoln's inaugural address in March 1861—seven days and seventeen hours. The 665 miles to Denver were run in two days and twenty-one hours, made possible by changing mounts more often.

By June of 1861 the Pacific Telegraph Company had organized

two groups of workmen, one under Edward Creighton building from Omaha west, the other supervised by James Gamble from Virginia City east. The first gang to reach Salt Lake was offered a substantial prize. Along the route the riders waved to their friendly rivals, the linesmen, engaged in rapidly displacing the Pony. By the end of the summer only a few hundred miles remained of the original run, and on October 24 the last link of the telegraph was completed, cutting off the most profitable business of the Pony Express.

In the meantime there were organizational changes. Holladay was to freeze out Russell, Majors and Waddell, who suffered a $200,000 loss in this glorious venture. Holladay in turn was to sell out to Wells, Fargo and Company. And then on October 25 the public was notified that the Pony Express would be discontinued from that date. The *Sacramento Union* published the following obituary:

"It is with regret we part with the Pony, but it seems to be considered by those who established the Express that it has accomplished its mission."

So ended the most romantic episode in the history of transportation in the Far West, the story of the *mochila* mail.

THE BATTLE OF THE GIANTS

HE BUTTERFIELD OVERLAND MAIL was highly successful, and yet it failed to appease those who favored a similar service over a central route. A regular wagon mail service from St. Joseph to Sacramento by way of Salt Lake City had kept going throughout the turbulent 'fifties, but the slow pace was heartbreaking for Westerners, who cried out for greater speed. Of course, the Pony Express had been established, but it was costly, and made no provision for the transportation of passengers. Advocates of a speeded-up service over the central plains foresaw the coming sectional clash, and they wanted to be prepared for the day when war might disrupt the grand but none-the-less vulnerable Butterfield Overland Mail. Moreover, business in many forms was on the increase all along the central trail. Stephen A. Douglas' "Squatter Sovereignty" opened the floodgates of settlement on the Kansas plains; the great Pike's Peak Gold Rush brought thousands of people into Colorado; the end of the "Mormon War" improved relations with Salt Lake City; and the discovery of the Comstock Lode caused other thousands, mostly Californians, to dash off to the desert mountains of Nevada. The Central West literally boomed with activity, and no matter what happened to Butterfield this region was entitled to fast, through, stage and mail service.

Whatever the federal government might do about mail contracts, the business future along the central overland trail to California was such as to attract the transportation interests. During 1859, for instance, there went into operation the important Leavenworth and Pike's Peak Express Company. In February 1860 there was chartered by Kansas Territory the Central Overland California and Pike's Peak Express Company, which concern absorbed the L. and P. P. Ex. Co.

The officers of this new company included the famous freighting trio of Russell, Majors and Waddell. It is not surprising that in the face of such competition George Chorpenning's contract for tortoise-paced service was annulled and in its place a new semimonthly contract granted to the new firm to be popularly known either as the Central Overland, or the C. O. C. and P. P. Ex. Co. Into the hands of this concern soon fell practically all important passenger mail service on the central route between the Missouri River and the Far West.

As national events neared a climax the next logical step was to secure daily service over the central route. Horace Greeley and Schuyler Colfax, both of whom had returned from their Western trips, advocated greater support of a speeded-up central overland service rather than encouragement to the ocean lines. Colfax was chairman of the important congressional Committee on Post Offices and Post Roads, and from this strategic position he introduced the Overland Mail Bill during March 1860. The measure was designed to have all mails carried overland in what would be daily twenty-day service. Other proposals followed. Soon the debate was on in full force and it continued for a year. At the end of this time, on March 2, 1861, a measure was passed with executive approval.

By this time seven states had already seceded from the Union, and in recognition of this the new law provided that "the Postmaster-General is hereby directed to discontinue the mail service on route 12578," meaning the Butterfield Line.

Service would be over a central route "from some point on the Missouri River connected with the East, to Placerville, California." Letter mail would be sent six days a week and in twenty days' time. There were other minor stipulations. For this entire service said contractors would receive $1,000,000 per year.

On the basis of this law a business deal was made whereby the C. O. C. and P. P. Ex. Co. (the Russell, Majors and Waddell concern) would offer to carry the mails east of Salt Lake City, and the Butterfield interests would take it between the Mormon capital and Placerville. With this arrangement the contract was let.

Service began July 1, 1861, and the first westbound mail and passengers arrived, without much ceremony, in San Francisco on the evening of July 18.

These were anxious days, and fears for the new service were expressed. Not least of these fears was the Indians. The red men of the plains, knowing full well that the Great White Father at Washington had his hands full, might attack the new stage line of the West. To forestall such action the War Department ordered out the cavalry from California to protect the line. As a result there were no attacks during 1861, although there were slight depredations from another source, namely, Confederate troops at Hannibal and St. Joseph.

On the whole the service was good. In spite of the war, decent weather permitting, the letter mail usually went through in twenty days. The first serious difficulties arose during the winter of 1861 when the heavy snows on the plains and in the high Sierra Nevada slowed up the drivers. Even so, Californians, especially northern Californians, refused to admit that the central route was not a practical one for all-year service. But the stages came through irregularly during that first cold winter.

The most serious trouble of all was, however, neither the Indians nor the weather. It was finance.

Throughout this period there had been lurking in the background the figure of a man now about to step into the open and demand his pound of flesh, Ben Holladay. Holladay was a typical product of the ruthless West. Born in Kentucky in 1820, he had gone to St. Louis as a lad of sixteen. Without the doubtful blessings of a formal education the energetic Ben found himself successively a store clerk, a liquor vendor, a tavern keeper, and, at twenty, postmaster and the proprietor of a small hotel in Weston, Missouri.

It was the Mexican War in 1846 that caused Ben Holladay to become interested in transportation, securing as he did a contract to supply General Stephen W. Kearny with wagons and foodstuffs. The California Gold Rush offered additional opportunities; and in this connection Holladay formed a partnership with Theodore W. Warner for hauling supplies to Salt Lake City, where their produce was sold at a good profit to westbound immigrants. In Utah Holladay used his money for the purchase of cattle, which he drove to California and sold to the Panama Steamship Company. He repeated this venture, while at the same time he organized some freighting concerns in California during the 'fifties. After the "Mormon War" of 1857 Holladay became associated with Russell, Majors and Waddell and in this connection capitalized the Pike's Peak Gold Rush in Colorado at the close of the decade. Thus with the outbreak of the Civil War and the resultant disruption of the Butterfield Overland Mail, it was Ben Holladay who was in a position, from the standpoint of both financial resources and personal experience, to exert his influence upon staging developments on the plains.

When in 1861 the C. O. C. and P. P. Ex. Co. ran into financial trouble, it was this man, the black-bearded dynamo, Ben Holladay, who advanced much-needed money, in return for which he received first mortgage on the line and on all the equipment of the company.

The day Holladay had secretly waited for came sooner than expected. In March 1862 the C. O. C. and P. P. Ex. Co. failed to meet expenses, and all assets of the firm were offered for sale at public auction in Atchison. It was on the occasion of this auction that Holladay, seeking as a mortgagor to protect his investment, made the highest bid of $100,000. By this transaction the irrepressible Holladay found himself in possession of over 1,200 miles of stage lines—albeit nonprofitable ones.

Holladay dared not and did not rest upon his oars. He hastily revamped his main line between Atchison and Salt Lake City. The name Overland Stage Line was adopted—in 1866 to be changed to Holladay Overland Mail & Express Company. Much new equipment was added, modern and up-to-date coaches were ordered from the Abbott-Downing Company, faster livestock was purchased, personnel changes were made, the main route itself was altered to provide cut-offs and to meet recent population shifts, and all along these routes Holladay built many new stations, such that the distance between any two of them was from ten to fifteen miles. Most important of all, he secured other favorable contracts from the United States government for carrying the mails over his line.

Moreover, this new king of Western staging was quick to capitalize the great flow of miners into the Inland Empire. It is known that as early as March 1864 Holladay had secured a mail contract and had plans laid for an extension of the Atchison-Salt Lake City line to run over the familiar Corinne Road from Salt Lake City to Virginia City, Montana Territory (300 miles); and on July 1, 1864, a triweekly service was actually begun which passed old Fort Hall. Later this service was extended to other mining towns in the Montana district.

Holladay did not stop here. In fact, his mail contract called for similar triweekly service between Salt Lake City, the Boise Valley, Walla Walla, Umatilla, and The Dalles. At any of the last three points passengers and mail could be transferred to steamers of the Oregon Steam Navigation Company for delivery at Portland, Oregon, or vice versa. Fort Hall again became an important junction in that the Idaho-, Washington-, and Oregon-bound stages there turned west from the aforementioned Salt Lake City-Montana route. The contract called for service over this section to begin September 30, 1864.

In its final organization as of 1866 the Holladay network was a far-flung and highly successful transportation system. Its line of stages commenced at Atchison on the Missouri River and extended westward 650 miles to Denver, then another 600 miles to Salt Lake City. From here one branch line extended 950 miles northwest to The Dalles, on the Columbia River, and a second reached out from the foregoing one for an added distance of 400 miles into Montana.

Twice each year Holladay personally made a hurried trip over his lines. He was a great showman, traveling in a luxurious coach pulled by the finest horses at great speed. Once he had himself driven from Salt Lake City to Atchison (1,250 miles) in what was a record time of six and one-half days. He had come originally from California, and his total time from San Francisco to Atchison was twelve days and two hours. The trip cost him an estimated $12,000 in damage to horses and equipment.

On the whole, Holladay was an efficient, though perhaps unscrupulous, manager, and in return for his efforts he received $650,000 a year from the federal government for hauling mails, in addition to revenue from hauling passengers and express.

One serious stumbling block stood in the way of Holladay's bid for complete monopoly of all the stagecoach business of the

West. This was Wells, Fargo and Company, which on July 1, 1861, the date service began, had acquired the Butterfield line. This, it will be recalled, had been transferred from the South and assigned to the route between Salt Lake City and Placerville. This Wells Fargo acquisition was not at all surprising in view of the close relationship between the Butterfield and Wells Fargo interests.

Supervision of this new Wells Fargo line fell to Louis McLane, the efficient general agent for the concern in the West, and to A. H. Barney of New York, the firm's president. McLane assumed special responsibility for the stretch between Folsom, then the eastern terminal of the railroad, and Carson City; whereas Barney personally represented the company between Carson City and Salt Lake City.

Between Folsom and Salt Lake City, then, Wells, Fargo and Company maintained fifty-three stage stations. At each station (in 1861) eight horses were kept for stages and two for Pony Express. Counting extras used for hauling supplies and special services, the total number of horses was 600, valued at about $125 apiece, or a total of $75,000. About fifty wagons and stagecoaches were put on the line at a cost of about $15,000, also 600 sets of harness costing $15,000, and road equipment costing about $125,000.

Under Wells Fargo management the routes of the drivers averaged about fifty miles each, and the wages were fixed at seventy-five dollars per month and board.

The official schedule between Sacramento and Salt Lake City —a distance of twenty-two miles from Sacramento to Folsom was traveled by train—required seven days, six and one-half hours. Mail over the route was heavy from the outset. During the first fifteen days of September 1861, for example, 14,163 letters were received at San Francisco via the Central Overland.

The Wells, Fargo and Company profited most from its express business, especially over that part of the route connecting California with the silver-boom town of Virginia City, Nevada. In order to exploit this business to the full, this concern organized what they called the Washoe Express and also established a large banking and express office at Virginia City. The need of the Nevada people for fresh foods made the transportation of such perishable commodities as butter, eggs, and fresh vegetables profitable. In return, large quantities of bullion were carried back from Nevada to San Francisco. In other quarters, too, Wells Fargo thrived. The Company's connections with the Pacific Northwest, especially with the British Columbia gold diggings, proved remunerative. In such areas, where the company did not operate its own equipment, it continued its policy of having connections with steamship companies and with stagecoach lines. One of the heaviest carriers of Wells Fargo Express was the Pacific Mail Steamship Company. Receipts rose steadily, and in 1862 they averaged about $40,000 per month.

So long as the eastern end of the central overland route remained in the hands of Russell, Majors and Waddell, the Wells Fargo firm entertained few fears concerning its transcontinental connections. But when on July 19, 1862, it learned that Ben Holladay had assumed the control and direct management of the line east of Salt Lake City, it experienced great uneasiness. What if the Holladay lines should refuse to carry Wells Fargo Express? Were they to be at the mercy of this ruthless opportunist?

The fears entertained by Wells, Fargo and Company were justified, for it was not long before troubles arose concerning the shipment of express over the Holladay facilities. Express concerns generally, and Wells Fargo in particular, began pressing Holladay for fixed through rates, and for rates for shorter distances on a *pro rata* basis; but Holladay refused to budge on this issue. He had the expressmen where he wanted them, so he thought, and he would fix his own rates.

This fight dragged on, but in 1866 the express interests brought matters to a climax by threatening to stock a line of their own between Salt Lake City and St. Joseph in direct competition with Holladay. When the irascible Holladay heard of this he is supposed to have burst out to his secretary: "Answer those express companies to stock and be damned."

Wells Fargo held one big trump card, however, and Holladay knew it. From the boxes of his own coaches he could plainly witness hundreds of Irish paddies methodically extending the Union Pacific Railroad westward across the prairies. He knew that, out in California and across the sagebrush valleys of Nevada, Chinese coolies were racing eastward in their construction of the

Central Pacific. Soon the twain would meet. And when that happened the great stagecoach empire of Ben Holladay would all but collapse.

As for Wells, Fargo and Company, they could, so he thought, sit tight. With the completion of the railroad the express company might make use of the rail facilities for transit purposes. Holladay had much to lose by continued resistance to overtures from the express concern.

For this reason and because Indian depredations were proving burdensome, Holladay realized that if he could get a fair offer for his holdings, the best thing to do would be to sell. And he reasoned well. On November 1, 1866, Louis McLane, representing Wells, Fargo and Company, purchased from the West's great "stagecoach king" the entire Holladay Overland Mail and Express system. For this Holladay received $1,500,000 in cash, $300,000 of Wells, Fargo and Company stock, a directorship in the latter firm, and market prices for hay and feed turned over to the express firm. In addition to becoming important in the banking field, Wells Fargo, by this transaction, came into control of practically all the stage and express lines west of the Missouri River.

Twelve days following the purchase, stockholders of Wells Fargo met and officially changed the corporate name of Holladay Overland Mail and Express Company to Wells, Fargo and Company. This was shortly followed by a program of expansion. The capital stock was increased to $10,000,000 and new areas and new services were added. For one thing, the company went more heavily into the field of "fast freight" as distinguished from express. For instance, in 1867 express rates from San Francisco to Washoe were twelve cents per pound and fast freight rates were seven cents per pound; express was hauled between San Francisco and Salt Lake City at sixty cents per pound, fast freight at fifty cents per pound. These rates were subsequently lowered.

Beginning in July 1868 the company campaigned for more passenger business and advertised the sale of passenger tickets for "across the continent via Pacific Railroad and Wells, Fargo and Company Stages." All who made this overland trip, according to one passenger, "agree in saying that a few days shaking up in one of Wells Fargo & Co.'s coaches is for most diseases worth all the medicine that ever doctor prescribed or unwilling patient swallowed." The fare from San Francisco to Chicago was $265.25; that to New York $290.20. The time required to New York was thirteen days.

More than ever, it seemed, Wells Fargo became identified with California and the West. The name came to be regarded, to use the words of one traveler, as an "institution as much a part of any western town as a billiard saloon and restaurant." There were those who complained because Wells Fargo had become a monopoly and therefore ceased to be interested in continued good service; but on the whole the complaints were few.

To the end, stage driving remained very much the same as in the heyday of the California Stage Company. Concord coaches continued to be used, four- and six-horse teams continued their gallop over bumpy dirt roads, and confident drivers continued to hold the reins.

Then came May 10, 1869. The two great railroad lines joined at Promontory Point. Before a motley crowd Leland Stanford drove the golden spike, and telegraph apparatus connected with this spike heralded to all Americans the completion of the first transcontinental railroad. Staging along the central route was for all intents and purposes over. A romantic, yet archaic, mode of travel gave way to a better.

As this event approached there was one great problem that concerned Wells, Fargo and Company. Would this company get the contract to handle the express aboard the new steam-driven coaches which soon would replace the horse-drawn Concords? One might have thought so; but, on the whole, this express-stage-coach-banking firm had not been any too friendly to the coming of the railroad. After all, the Wells Fargo of the West seemed inseparable from the stagecoach era. There was no telling what the railroad era might do to the express business. As for the stagecoach business, it could never compete with the iron horse.

So far as the Union Pacific Company was concerned Wells Fargo was out of luck. The exclusive privilege of handling express over this line went to the United States Express Company.

Then what about the Central Pacific? To the surprise, if not consternation, of most interested parties the Central Pacific Railroad Company, on September 25, 1869, granted the Pacific Express Company, and not the Wells, Fargo and Company, the exclusive privilege of handling express over its facilities for a period of ten years. The chief reason for this arrangement may well be explained by the fact that the Central Pacific Railroad Company owned three-fifths of the stock of the Pacific Express concern.

Such a situation seemed ruinous to Wells Fargo, and officers of the company lost no time in seeking an arrangement with their competitors. A joint meeting of directors of both companies was held at Omaha on October 4. D. O. Mills and Lloyd Tevis were at this meeting representing the Pacific Express; William G. Fargo, Charles Fargo, and A. H. Barney were there in person to represent the badly cornered but none-the-less powerful Wells, Fargo and Company.

At this momentous Omaha conference Wells, Fargo and Company was given, for a consideration of $5,000,000, the exclusive privilege of handling express over the Central Pacific, and the retirement from business of the Pacific Express Company was arranged.

A stormy meeting of Wells, Fargo and Company stockholders followed on November 25 to discuss how to raise the necessary $5,000,000 with which to conclude the Omaha transaction. Accounts vary somewhat, but it would appear that this huge sum was produced by increasing the capital stock of the company from $10,000,000 to $15,000,000. The price paid seemed to some of the stockholders at the time like financial highjacking; but the decision proved sound from the long-range point of view. As the Central Pacific, which later became the Southern Pacific, Railroad system expanded throughout the West and on south into Mexico, Wells, Fargo and Company expanded with it. Had Wells Fargo not made this investment, its express services might well have gone the way of its stagecoach line into the limbo of pleasant and exciting memories.

But this has taken us into the new and more modern age of rails. With the coming of railroads in California, the stagecoach, the Pony, the horse-drawn express, and even river steamers began giving way to a faster and more modern form of transportation. The change was slow but inevitable, and with the turn of the century California could have read with a nostalgia for olden days the reminiscent lines of Sidney Dyer:

"The old stagecoach, as it came, of old,
    "Each idler roused with its noisy din;
"With cracking whip, how it briskly rolled,
    · "With conscious pride, to the village inn!
"But now it stands in the stable-yard,
    "With dusty seats and a rusty tire,
"And we this friend of our youth discard,
    "For railway cars and a steed of fire;
" . . . ."

BIBLIOGRAPHICAL NOTE

THE MATERIALS UPON WHICH THIS BOOK
has been written are too numerous to list. They include contemporary
manuscripts, newspapers, periodicals, printed government documents,
monographs, court records, timetables, broadsides, express franks, pic-
tures, and advertisements in possession of the Wells Fargo Bank and
Union Trust Company Historical Museum in San Francisco, the Stanford
University Library, the Bancroft Library, the Henry E. Huntington Library, the California State Library at Sacramento, and the Indiana University Library. The personnel of these institutions were generous in
making materials available to the author.

Moreover, this book is based upon extensive wanderings over California's mountain roads and trails and through ghost towns, upon exami-
nation of what remains of the pre-rail age—coaches, saddles, guns, express boxes, and the like—and upon interesting chats with oldtimers,
without whom the flavor of yesteryears would have been difficult to
capture.

SELECTED BOOKS OF REFERENCE

William Banning and George Hugh Banning, *Six Horses* (New York, 1930).

Mrs. D. B. Bates, *Incidents on Land and Water; or, Four Years on the
Pacific Coast* (Boston, 1860).

Mae Hélène Bacon Boggs, comp., *My Playhouse Was a Concord Coach* (Oakland, 1942).

Samuel Bowles, *Our New West* (New York, 1869).

Glenn D. Bradley, *The Story of the Pony Express* (Chicago, 1913).

J. Ross Browne, *Adventures in the Apache Country* (New York, 1869).

Arthur Chapman, *The Pony Express* (New York, 1932).

Stanton A. Coblentz, *Villains and Vigilantes* (New York, 1936).

Alonzo Delano, *Life on the Plains and Among the Diggings* (Auburn and
Buffalo, 1854).

H. R. Driggs, *The Pony Express Goes Through* (New York, 1935).

J. V. Frederick, *Ben Holladay: The Stagecoach King* (Glendale, California,
1940).

Horace Greeley, *An Overland Journey* (New York, 1860).

LeRoy R. Hafen, *The Overland Mail, 1849–1869* (Cleveland, 1926).

Alvin Harlow, *Old Waybills: The Romance of the Express Companies* (New York, 1934).

Hinton R. Helper, *The Land of Gold: Reality versus Fiction* (Baltimore, 1855).

Rockwell D. Hunt and William S. Ament, *Oxcart to Airplane* (Los Angeles, 1929).

[Henry V. Huntley], *California: Its Gold and Its Inhabitants* (London, 1856).

Joseph Henry Jackson, *Tintypes in Gold: Four Studies in Robbery* (New York, 1939).

William Kelly, *An Excursion to California,* 2 vols. (London, 1851).

[Walter Barnes Lang], *The First Overland Mail: Butterfield Trail* (n. p., 1940).

Alexander Majors, *Seventy Years on the Frontier* (Chicago, 1893).

Frank Marryat, *Mountains and Molehills, or, Recollections of a Burnt Journal* (New York and London, 1855).

Frank A. Root and William E. Connelley, *The Overland Stage to California* (Topeka, 1901).

William R. Ryan, *Personal Adventures in Upper and Lower California, 1848–49,* 2 vols. (London, 1850).

A. L. Stimson, *History of the Express Companies* . . . . (New York, 1858).

Mark Twain, *Roughing It,* 2 vols., any edition.

William Lightfoot Visscher, *A Thrilling and Truthful History of the Pony Express* (Chicago, 1908).

Henry Wells, *Sketch of the Rise, Progress, and Present Condition of the Express System* (Albany, New York, 1864).

Neill C. Wilson, *Treasure Express: Epic Days of the Wells Fargo* (New York, 1936).

Ernest A. Wiltsee, *The Pioneer Miner and the Pack Mule Express* (San Francisco, 1931).

Oscar Osburn Winther, *Express and Stagecoach Days in California* (Stanford University, 1936, 1938).

Lyle H. Wright and Josephine M. Bynum, eds., *The Butterfield Overland Mail,* by Waterman L. Ormsby (San Marino, 1942).

INDEX

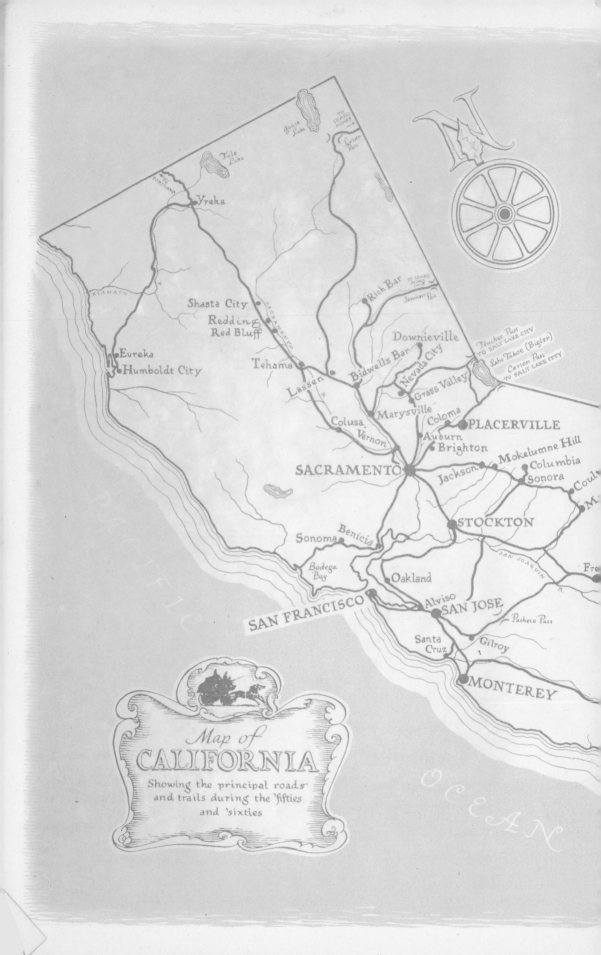

Map of
CALIFORNIA
Showing the principal roads
and trails during the 'fifties
and 'sixties